THE 15-MINUTE CHINESE GOURMET

THE 15-MINUTE
CHINESE GOURMET

◆

Elizabeth Chiu King

Photographs by Janine Menlove
Illustrations by Barbara Fiore

Macmillan Publishing Company ◆ New York
Collier Macmillan Publishers ◆ London

To the Creator
for His delicious bounty on this planet Earth
and
to the three creatures He has given to me
to nourish with food and love:
Albert, my husband, and our two sons, Albert, Jr. and Tom

Macmillan Publishing Company
866 Third Avenue, New York, N.Y. 10022
Collier Macmillan Canada, Inc.

Library of Congress Cataloging-in-Publication Data
Chiu King, Elizabeth, 1938–
The 15-minute Chinese gourmet.
Includes index.
1. Cookery, Chinese. I. Title. II. Title: Fifteen minute Chinese gourmet.
TX724.5.C5C564 1986   641.5951   85-23184
ISBN 0-02-563130-6

Macmillan books are available at special discounts for bulk purchases for sales promotions, premiums, fund-raising, or educational use. For details, contact:

Special Sales Director
Macmillan Publishing Company
866 Third Avenue
New York, N.Y. 10022

10 9 8 7 6 5 4 3 2 1
Book design by Joe Marc Freedman
Printed in the United States of America

CONTENTS

◈ Listing of Recipes ◈

◇ *Listing of Recipes* ◇

PREFACE

Writing this cookbook has been a challenge—to choose a few recipes from the thousands of dishes that are part of the splendor and legacy of Chinese cooking. A challenge to adapt the recipes to a short time span as well as to the American kitchen. A challenge to limit Chinese ingredients to no more than 12.

All these recipes are authentic Chinese dishes, but I have simplified and adapted them for your kitchen. You will be able to cook them in very little time. Except for the *staples* and some desserts, these recipes can be prepared in 15 minutes. For convenience and the sake of retaining familiar terms, I have not adhered to a single system of romanization. The Chinese terms used in this book are a mixture of the Wades-Giles, Yale, and Pinyin systems.

Here are some hints to help you succeed:

- Organize to achieve the best results in the allotted time.
- Use the proper equipment to save time and energy.
- Follow the Game Plan (p.5), Flow Chart (p.15), and Time-savers (p.6) carefully.
- Assemble all your ingredients and equipment before cooking and place them within easy reach.
- Prepare the *Before you start* steps ahead of time, even several hours or overnight, if you can.

I have been collecting and testing these recipes for 30 years in my own kitchen and in my cooking classes. They have also been tested and retested by many cooks, from novices to gourmets.

It is with pride and love that I offer them to you.

Confucius once said, "Give a man a fish and you feed him for a day; teach him to fish and you feed him for life." I hope this book will teach you how to cook and eat the Chinese way. Eat well, stay healthy, and be happy.—ELIZABETH

ACKNOWLEDGMENTS

Corinne Abatt, for believing in me from the start.

Ah Woo, my amah, in loving memory, for teaching my mother, who in turn, taught me to love eating and cooking.

Ellen Ahern, for maintaining the vertical file.

Margaret Allen, for encouragement and professional writing advice.

Michelle Andonian, for photographic friendship.

Evelyn Cairns, for advice and editorial articles.

Frank Chiu, my father, in loving memory, for teaching me to strive for excellence.

Rowena Luk Chiu, my mother, for life, nurturing, and love.

Grace Chu, for listening with love and patience.

Patricia L. Cornett, my Detroit editor, for excellent professional help and for testing the recipes.

Father Fergus Cronin, S.J., for introducing me to Albert, logic, and India.

Father Horace deAngelis, for believing in the pursuit of excellence.

Nona Dreyer, for brainstorming and sharing my trials and tribulations.

Mother Emma, in loving memory, for happy days at St. Mary's.

Jeanette Fehner, for nurturing and support.

John Flatter, for brainstorming and listening with patience.

Charles Hsieh, for his Chinese calligraphy.

Chen-ai Hsieh, for brainstorming and encouragement.

Helen E. King, my mother-in-law, for listening, news clippings, love, and Albert.

Yu-Lo King, my father-in-law, in loving memory, for his example of dedication and patience.

Jonathon L. Lazear, my ace agent, for originating the idea and for his confidence in me.

Rick Leffke, for showing me how "to smell the flowers" along the way.

Bob and Faye Levine, for judicious critique of the recipes and suggestions.

Father Thomas Liang, in loving memory, for "sunsets."

Dan Longone, for his expertise on wine.

Jan Longone, for nourishing me with books, advice, and tea.

David Louie, for seeing the "swan" in me.

Spencer Lowe, for giving and sharing his artistic talents.

David McCarthy, for encouraging me to reach for the stars.

Jack McCarthy, for sharing his love for food and Friday Feasts.

Janine Menlove, for her exquisite photographs.

Mother Piera, for challenging my mind and spirit at St. Mary's.

Joan and Michael Rabins, for their judicious testing and critique of the recipes.

Mary Frances Ray, for nurturing with love.

Louise Schlaff, for launching me on my writing career.

Father Jim and my friends at St. Beatrice's Church, for testing the recipes.

My colleagues and students at Henry Ford Community College, for helping me in more ways than one, including testing the recipes.

My students at Oakland Community College, for testing the recipes.

My friends, far and near, for love and encouragement, especially Jane Chao, Bertha Cohen, Pat Doline, Armand Gebert, Jessica Goodwin, Mildred Jeffrey, Jane Kenyon, Anne Lalas, Eileen Liang, Ginka Ortega, Theresa Shen, Lillian and John Siak, Guy and Judy Stern, Wendy Thoryn, Betty Tyson, and Elaine Watson.

My sisters, Mimi, Maria, Shirley, and their families, for love and support.

My sisters-in-law, Shirley and Lucy, Anna and Janice for love and support.

And above all, to my editors at Macmillan, Arlene Friedman and Melinda Corey, for their patience and assistance in many ways.

INTRODUCTION

Do you enjoy Chinese food but think it is too time-consuming and difficult to prepare?

Do you work all day but like to put an appetizing meal on the table in the evening?

Do you like authentic Chinese food, not chop suey, and want to serve delicious Chinese dishes you can prepare quickly?

Do you want to improve your health and cut down on cholesterol and fat?

Do you get tired of eating out every night?

Do you want to stop paying for expensive carry-out food?

The *15-Minute Chinese Gourmet* is the cookbook for you. It combines the best of all worlds. It offers authentic Chinese recipes that are fast, fresh, flavorful, and healthy.

These recipes

- can be prepared and cooked in just 15 minutes. The staples take longer, but once cooked they are springboard recipes which you can use to create others.
- retain their flavor and nutritional value without sacrifice to speed.
- are adapted for you, the American cook. Cutting is kept to a minimum, and many cooking techniques are simple and familiar.
- can be cooked in your American kitchen with your own pots or pans.
- call for the freshest ingredients you can find.
- use no more than a dozen Chinese ingredients, including condiments and dried foods.

These recipes are fast, fresh, flavorful, and healthy.

1

FEATURES

Scope

Appetizers, Entrees, Salads and Vegetables, Rice and Noodles, and Desserts.

Authentic but simple recipes, adapted from over 30 years of cooking.

Emphasis

Quick to prepare, but good tasting dishes with eye appeal.

Light and healthy, low-calorie and low-cholesterol.

High in fiber.

Format

Each recipe has the same format and easy-to-follow directions.

Left hand column: Ingredients, Marinade, Seasoning, Sauce, Binder, Equipment, all listed in the order used.

Right hand column: Numbered directions with simple clear instructions.

Recipes arranged in order of complexity, from simple to complex.

Ingredients

All meats, seafood, and vegetables are available from local supermarkets.

Chinese ingredients are limited to 12, including condiments and dried foods These are usually available from Chinese or Oriental markets or by mail from other stores (see p. 125 for mail-order stores).

Fresh ingredients preferred, but frozen vegetables may be substituted.

Canned products are used sparingly.

Special cuts of meat, seafood, and poultry are needed to save time and minimize cutting.

Techniques

Completely adapted to the American kitchen.

Minimum cutting.

Simple marinades, seasonings, and sauces.

Chinese cooking methods are stir-tossing (stir-frying), steaming, cold-tossing, and steeping. Familiar cooking methods include baking, boiling, broiling, deep-frying, frying, pan-frying, parboiling, pickling, and roasting.

Utensils

Regular pots and pans, including skillet.

Conventional and microwave ovens, food processor, and blender.

Woks, steamers, and rice cookers are useful and convenient but not necessary.

Substitutes given.

A Chinese cleaver is handy, but a sharp kitchen knife will do.

Small portions of meat, poultry, and seafood—usually no more than 4 ounces per serving.

Each recipe usually serves 4.

Two dishes can easily make a whole meal for 4 people, together with a rice or noodle dish.

See Suggested Menus, p. 121.

⬦ *How to Be a Successful*
15-Minute Chinese Gourmet Cook ⬦

Game Plan

Plan and organize for speed and best results!

Stock up on your Chinese Cupboard (p. 7).

Stock up on your American Cupboard (p. 13).

Make quick stops at the supermarket to pick up fresh ingredients.

Assemble the necessary equipment and supplies (p. 14) and store in a convenient place.

Keep appliances in good working order, keep knives and scissors sharp.

Cook the staples (S) on weekends or whenever you have extra time, then refrigerate or freeze until ready to use.

Use timesavers (TS) on p. 15. They are the key to your success.

On busy workdays, cook 15-minute recipes. Plan accordingly. Many recipes have an added *Before you start* section of preliminary steps. These steps can be done ahead of time, sometimes as much as a day or a few hours in advance.

Check Flow Chart.

Enjoy in good health!

Flow Chart for a Successful 15-Minute Chinese Gourmet

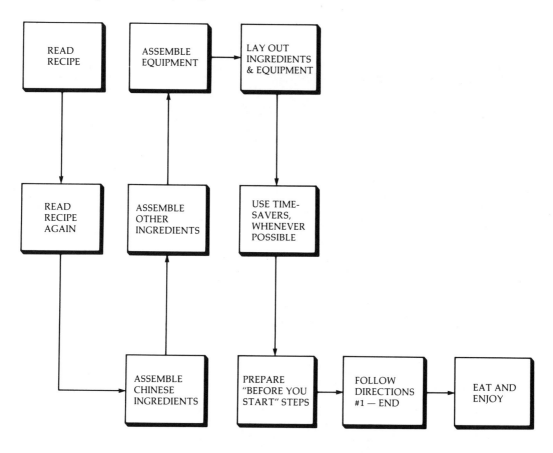

❖ *The Chinese Cupboard* ❖

The 12 Chinese ingredients needed for *The 15-Minute Chinese Gourmet*:

Agar-agar strips (dried transparent seaweed)

Cellophane noodles (bean thread or transparent noodles)

Chinese dried black mushrooms (dried shiitake mushrooms)

Crunchy mushrooms (commercially known as *won yee* or *cloud ears*)

Five-spice powder

Hoisin sauce

Hunan chili paste (hot doubanjiang)

Litchis (lichees, lychees, or lichinuts)

Oyster sauce

Sesame seed oil

Shrimp chips (prawn crackers or lobster chips)

Straw mushrooms

12 Chinese Ingredients: Description, Storage and Shelf Life, Substitution, Recommended Brands and Size

There are as many variables in Chinese canned or bottled goods as there are brands. What's more, some brands may not be available in all cities or areas of the country. If the recommended brands are available, try them and compare.

AGAR-AGAR STRIPS (dried transparent seaweed) 大膠菜

Description: The Chinese equivalent of gelatin. Usually packaged in long dried strips, it is used in salads or in desserts. As an

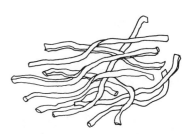

ingredient in salads, it is soaked in cold water, drained, and seasoned. When used in desserts, it has to be boiled and dissolved. It has a crunchy texture and, unlike its Western counterpart, will not dissolve at room temperature. High in protein and low in cholesterol.

Storage and shelf life: In their dried state, agar-agar strips will keep indefinitely when wrapped and stored on the shelf. Soaked agar-agar strips can be kept, drained, in a covered container, for at least a week in the refrigerator.

Substitution: Unflavored gelatin can be used for agar-agar strips in desserts. No substitution for agar-agar strips in salads. Agar-agar flakes or powder is not acceptable.

Recommended brands and size: Any Chinese or Japanese brand acceptable; buy small (2- to 4-ounce) packages of dried strips.

CELLOPHANE NOODLES (bean thread or transparent noodles)

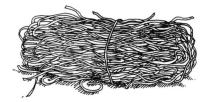

Description: Made from mung bean flour, they are used in soups, stir-fried dishes, or salads. Sold dried and bundled, they become transparent when soaked. When cooked, they absorb the flavor of the main ingredients. When deep-fried, they puff up and are often used as a garnish or as an ingredient in salads.

Storage and shelf life: In their dried form, they can be stored indefinitely on the shelf. After being soaked in water, they can be kept, drained, in a covered container, for about a week in the refrigerator. When deep-fried, they can be stored in an air-tight container and kept in the refrigerator for about a week.

Substitution: None

Recommended brands and sizes: Any Chinese brand acceptable; buy small (1½ or 2-ounce) packages.

CHINESE DRIED BLACK MUSHROOMS (dried shiitake mushrooms) 冬菇

Description: Dried and very lightweight, these mushrooms are actually dark brown in color. They must first be soaked in warm or hot water before they can be sliced and cooked. Though expensive, they are delicious and add flavor, texture, and variety to any dish of meat, poultry, or vegetables.

Storage and shelf life: Dried black mushrooms will keep for months when stored in a tightly-covered container or plastic bag in the refrigerator. Soaked mushrooms can be kept, drained, in a covered container for at least a week in the refrigerator.

Substitution: Fresh shiitake mushrooms.

Recommended brands and size: Any Chinese or Japanese brand acceptable; buy small (2- or 4-ounce) packages.

CRUNCHY MUSHROOMS (won yee or cloud ears) 雲耳

Description: Dried and very lightweight, they must first be soaked in warm or hot water until soft and have expanded to four times their original size. Their crunchy texture, irregular shapes, and brown color add an unusual dimension to cooked dishes.

Storage and shelf life: In their dried form, crunchy mushrooms will keep indefinitely, when stored in a tightly-covered container on the shelf. Soaked mushrooms can be kept, in cold water, in a covered container for at least a week in the refrigerator.

Substitution: None

Recommended brands and size: Any Chinese brand acceptable; buy small (2-ounce) packages.

FIVE-SPICE POWDER 五香粉

Description: A fragrant red-brown powder made from the combination of star anise, peppercorn, fennel, cloves, and cinnamon.

Storage and shelf life: Will keep for months when stored in a tightly-covered jar on the shelf.

Substitution: None

Recommended brands and size: Any Chinese brand acceptable; buy small (2-ounce) packages.

HOISIN SAUCE 海鮮醬

Description: A velvety thick, red-brown sweet sauce made from wheat flour, soy beans, sugar, garlic, chili, and vinegar. It can be used as a dipping sauce or as a cooking condiment combined with meat, seafood, or tofu.

Storage and shelf life: When refrigerated and kept in a clean, tightly-covered jar it can be stored for months.

Substitution: None

Recommended brands and size: Koon Chun or Hop Sing Lung; usually packaged in 16-ounce jars or cans.

HUNAN CHILI PASTE (hot doubanjiang) 湖南辣椒醬

Description: A pungent, fiery hot condiment used in Sichuan and Hunan dishes. It is made from soy beans, salt, spices, fagara peppers, garlic, and sesame seed oil.

Storage and Shelf life: When refrigerated and kept in a tightly-covered jar, it can be stored for months.

Substitution: Any other brand of Chinese hot paste is acceptable. Different brands vary in intensity of hotness. Experiment for best results.

Recommended brands and size: Kuang Ta Hsiang; buy small (4-ounce) jars.

LITCHIS (lichees, lychees, lichinuts)

Description: Sweet, white, fleshy fruit, sold in cans and used primarily in desserts and in ices. They can also be cooked with meat, fowl, or seafood.

Storage and shelf life: Once the can has been opened, store unused portion with its juice in a covered container in refrigerator for a week.

Substitution: Fresh litchis preferred, when available.

Recommended brands and size: Any Chinese brand acceptable; usually packaged in 20-ounce cans.

OYSTER SAUCE 蠔油

Description: Made from soy sauce, seasonings, and a touch of oyster, Oyster sauce enriches and blends flavors while imparting a smooth velvety texture.

Storage and shelf life: When stored in a tightly-covered bottle in the refrigerator, it will keep for months.

Substitution: None

Recommended brands and size: Hop Sing Lung or Lee Kum Kee; usually packaged in 18-ounce bottles.

SESAME SEED OIL 蘇油

Description: Made from toasted sesame seeds. Sesame seed oil is not used as a cooking oil, but more as a flavoring agent, and definitely as part of the dressing for Chinese salads. It masks fish tastes without destroying the seafood flavor.

Storage and shelf life: Will keep for months in a tightly-covered bottle on the shelf.

Substitution: None. The pale variety available from Middle Eastern stores is not acceptable.

Recommended brands and size: Kadoya brand preferred; other Chinese or Japanese brands acceptable. Buy small (6-ounce) bottles.

SHRIMP CHIPS (prawn crackers or lobster chips) 蝦片

Description: Thin, white, or pastel-colored rounds of dried dough made from flour and a touch of shrimp (or lobster). When deep-fried, they expand and look like potato chips. They are wonderful by themselves or as an appetizer, snack, or garnish.

Storage and shelf life: Dried, they will keep on the shelf for months. Store unused dried chips in tightly-sealed plastic bags. Store fried chips in a tight container or plastic bag at room temperature. They keep for several days.

Substitution: None

Recommended brands and size: Any Chinese brand acceptable; usually packaged in ½-pound packages.

STRAW MUSHROOMS 草菇

Description: Cultivated from beds of rice straws in China, these small brown mushrooms are as delicate-tasting as they are attractive. Sold in cans, they come in two kinds, peeled or unpeeled. I prefer the *small and peeled* straw mushrooms.

Storage and shelf life: Once the can has been opened, store unused portion in cold water in a covered container in refrigerator. Will keep for at least a week.

Substitution: Fresh straw mushrooms preferred when available; canned button mushrooms are acceptable.

Recommended brands and size: Any Chinese brand acceptable; usually packaged in 15-ounce cans.

◈ *The American Cupboard* ◈

Baking soda
Black pepper
Cornstarch
Cream of tartar
Dijon mustard
Dried hot red peppers
Dried onion flakes
Dry peppercorns
Dry sherry, gin, or vodka
Honey

Ketchup
Salt
Soy sauce (Kikkoman or Wei
  Chuan brands recommended)
Sugar
Unflavored gelatin
Untoasted sesame seeds
Vinegar; cider, white, or wine
White pepper
Worcestershire sauce

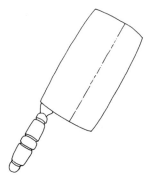

Standard equipment in an American kitchen

6- or 8-quart saucepot with lid
4-quart saucepot with lid
2-quart saucepot with lid
1½-quart saucepot with lid
10-inch skillet with lid
deep-fryer (optional)
11 x 17-inch baking sheet
11 x 17-inch baking pan
9 x 13-inch baking pan
8 x 8-inch baking pan
cookie sheets
baking rack
electric blender/mixer
food processor
sharp kitchen knife
paring knife/peeler
kitchen shears
large spoon/spatula
rubber spatula
wooden spoon
slotted spoon
soup ladle
wire mesh strainer
colander or strainer
grater and tongs
8-inch bamboo skewers
pastry brush
1½-inch thick cutting board
8-inch heat-proof plate with
  sides
9-inch sq. plastic container
  with lid

ice cube trays
tray for ingredients
serving platter
timer
cups or small bowls
medium and large bowls
metal bowls
measuring cups
measuring spoons

Chinese equipment (optional)

14-inch wok with lid, stainless
  or carbon steel
Chinese cleaver for cutting
6-cup electric rice cooker
Chinese wire strainer
13-inch Chinese steamer (or
  improvised steamer using a
  steamer rack and 14-inch wok
  or 4-quart saucepot with lid)
bamboo chopsticks

Supplies

kitchen gloves
paper towels, wax paper
Heavy-duty aluminum foil
plastic wrap
sealable plastic pouches
tightly-sealed jars or
  containers with lids

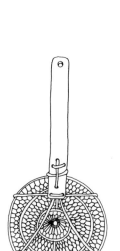

◈ *Timesavers* ◈

Garlic

1. Peel several heads of garlic by mashing with the flat side of a Chinese cleaver or a heavy knife.

2. Place peeled cloves in food processor and fine-mince. Or chop fine with Chinese cleaver or knife.

3. Store minced garlic in a jar with a tight lid and add enough corn, vegetable, or safflower oil to cover.

4. Minced garlic can be kept indefinitely in the refrigerator, while the garlic may age and turn brown, its quality and flavor will remain intact.

1 large clove of garlic = ½ teaspoon minced garlic

Gingerroot

SLICED

1. Wash, dry, and thin-slice a section of gingerroot into ⅛-inch wide slices.

2. Peeling is not necessary. If you prefer to peel the gingerroot, use a parer.

3. Place slices in a jar with a tight lid.

4. Add ¼ cup dry sherry, gin, or vodka.

5. When refrigerated, sliced ginger will keep indefinitely.

each slice = size of a 50-cent piece

GRATED

1. Grate a section of peeled gingerroot.

2. Store grated ginger in a covered jar with a tight lid.

3. Add several tablespoons of dry sherry, gin, or vodka.

½ teaspoon grated gingerroot = 1 slice
Ginger powder is not acceptable as a substitute, for its flavor is flat.

Scallions

1. Wash 1 bunch of scallions with green tops, drain, and dry well with paper towels.

2. Remove and discard roots.

3. Fine-dice scallions with green tops into ⅛-inch pieces with Chinese cleaver or knife.

4. Store diced scallions in a covered jar in the refrigerator. Processed this way, diced scallions will keep for several weeks.

1 scallion = 2 tablespoons of diced scallions

Chinese Dried Black Mushrooms

1. Soak 8 to 12 small or medium Chinese dried black mushrooms, caps down, in medium bowl in 2 cups warm water for at least 20 minutes.

2. When they are soft and pliable, squeeze dry. Save mushroom water to use in soups or sauces in separate container, if preferred.

3. Cut off and discard stems. Soaked mushrooms can be kept, drained, in a covered container or jar for at least a week in the refrigerator.

Crunchy Mushrooms (Won Yee or Cloud Ears)

1. Soak 2 tablespoons crunchy mushrooms in medium bowl in 2 cups warm water for at least 5 minutes.

2. When they have expanded to 4 times their original size and are soft, squeeze dry. Discard soaking water.

3. Remove hard particles from mushrooms.

4. Crunchy mushrooms can be stored, in covered container or jar, in refrigerator for at least a week.

5. If you are using them in Hot and Sour Soup (p. 51), shred finely and store in refrigerator until ready to use.

1 tablespoon dried crunchy mushrooms = ¼ cup soaked crunchy mushrooms

Fried Cellophane Noodles

1. Heat 3 cups of corn, vegetable, or safflower oil almost to smoking, about 375°.

2. Unwrap and drop in 1 package (2-ounces) cellophane noodles.

3. Within 3 seconds, the noodles will puff up and turn white and crunchy.

4. With slotted spoon or wire mesh strainer, turn noodles over and deep-fry for several seconds.

5. Remove from hot oil and drain on paper towels.

6. Use as garnish for dishes, e.g., Hunan Beef with Potato Sticks (p. 58) or Ants on the Hill (p. 56), in Crunchy Noodle Salad (p. 90), or Chinese Gourmet Salad (p. 91), or as garnish for soups.

7. May be stored in a tightly-covered container for about a week.

2 ounces dried cellophane noodles = 5 cups fried noodles

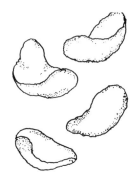

Shrimp Chips

1. Heat 3 cups corn, vegetable, or safflower oil almost to smoking, about 375°.

2. Drop in a handful of dried shrimp chips.

3. Within 5 seconds, they will puff up.

4. Remove immediately with slotted spoon or wire mesh strainer and drain on paper towels.

5. Use as garnish for dishes, e.g., Mandarin Roast Duck (p. 28) or No-work Chicken (p. 26), or as a snack.

6. Fried chips can be stored in a tightly-covered can or plastic bag for a few days without losing their crunchiness. Store unused portion of dried chips in tightly-sealed plastic bags.

1 package (½ pound) = 4 cups dried chips (each cup = about 50 chips)

◇ *Cooking Ingredients* ◇

COOKING OIL   Although peanut oil and lard are widely used in China, I have chosen corn, vegetable, or safflower oil for nutrition and convenience. These oils are low in cholesterol, easy to use, and readily available.

COOKING WINE   In many years of cooking, I have discovered that flavoring meats and seafood with a good dry sherry or good liquor (gin or vodka, which is inexpensive but good) adds to the overall richness of the dish. Even a teetotaler can produce satisfying results from cooking with liquor because the alcohol evaporates during the cooking process. It imparts richness and heightens flavors.

SOUP STOCK   Chicken or vegetable bouillon cubes are not recommended. They are too salty or not rich enough to produce the highest quality. Canned broth is an acceptable substitute. But homemade chicken or vegetable stock is the best base for recipes calling for them. When you have extra time, make up a batch and freeze the stock according to directions (p. 22).

AMOUNT OF SEASONING   The amount of salt and sugar called for in these recipes is flexible. Changing the amount of salt or sugar will not change the quality of the finished dish, *provided* the other seasonings are not changed. If you are used to more flavorful dishes, you can add a little more soy sauce, salt, or sugar.

AMOUNT OF COOKING OIL   The amount of oil listed in each recipe is based on the use of standard cookware. If you use Teflon-coated skillets and saucepots, you may cut down on the amount of oil. Experiment for best results.

AMOUNT OF CHILI PASTE   In recipes calling for hot chili paste, the degree of hotness varies: fiery hot (2 to 3 tablespoons), medium hot (1 to 1½ tablespoons), mild (½ tablespoon). Different brands of chili paste vary in intensity. Experiment for best results.

SOY SAUCE   Different brands vary in intensity and quality. My favorite brands are Kikkoman and Wei Chuan.

MSG   MSG is not used in any of the recipes. Instead, ½ teaspoon sugar will enhance the flavor of vegetables and meats.

◈ *Cutting and Cooking Techniques* ◈

To save time, I have reduced the cutting on these recipes to a minimum.

STRAIGHT-SLICING   The ingredient is cut perpendicular to the broad side of the knife. The slices are quite thin, ranging from ¼-inch to ⅛-inch in thickness.

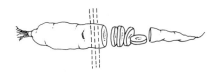

DIAGONAL-SLICING The ingredient is cut at a 45-degree angle to the broad side of the knife. The slices are usually ⅛ to ¼-inch thick.

JULIENNE-CUTTING Ingredients are cut into uniform strips, about ¼-inch thick. First, straight or diagonally slice the food into ¼-inch wide pieces. Let slices fall neatly into overlapping stacks like a flat staircase. Cut crosswise into ¼-inch wide strips at regular intervals.

CUBING First straight-slice into 1- or ½-inch wide strips, then cut into 1- or ½-inch cubes.

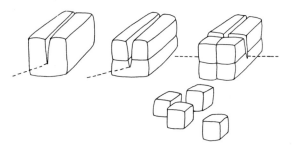

DICING Cut food lengthwise into ½- or ¼-inch strips, then into pea-size dices.

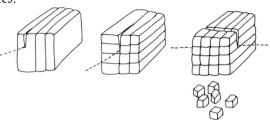

Most of the cooking techniques are familiar ones: baking, boiling, broiling, deep-frying, pan-frying, parboiling, pickling, and roasting.

Four Chinese techniques are used in these recipes:

STIR-FRYING OR STIR-TOSSING   Blitz-cooking on high heat. Ingredients are usually cut into uniform sizes (juliennes, cubes, dices, or slices), then quickly tossed and stirred in a little hot oil together with some basic seasonings. You should have all ingredients and seasonings within easy reach. Then you have to work fast, for vegetables and meats cut into small strips or pieces cook very quickly. The technique is similar to tossing a salad, except that it is done over high heat.

STEAMING   A process in which ingredients are placed in a heat-proof dish and gently cooked over boiling water in a covered steamer or pot. The boiling water is kept away from direct contact with the food. The hot steam that rises from the water is the cooking agent. If you steam food regularly, a 13-inch aluminum steamer is a good investment. The bottom pot holds enough boiling water to cook the food quickly, while the two racks with large perforated holes allow the steam to penetrate quickly. Using an improvised steamer will take longer to prepare the food because the low water level in the pot will add to the cooking time.

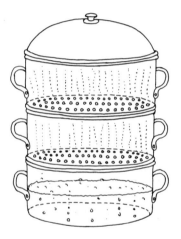

COLD-TOSSING   Mixing several ingredients, raw, cooked, or a combination of both, with seasonings. It is similar to tossing a salad, and the finished dish is often served cold.

STEEPING   A process in which a good broth is used as the cooking agent. When the broth comes to a boil, the ingredients are added and boiled for 5 to 10 minutes. The covered pot is then removed from the heat and left to stand covered while its contents slowly cook (4 to 6 hours). The resulting texture of meat or fowl is very tender.

2

RECIPES

◇ *The Staples* ◇

Basic Chicken Stock

Ingredients

*4 pounds chicken carcass and
    bones or 4 pound fryer or
    stewing chicken*
12 cups (6 pints) cold water
(TS) *4 slices gingerroot, each about the
    size of a 50-cent piece*
*4 scallions with green tops, cut
    into 2-inch lengths*
*½ cup dry sherry, gin, or vodka,
    optional*
1 teaspoon salt
½ teaspoon white pepper

Equipment

measuring spoons and cups
large spoon
6- or 8-quart saucepot with lid
Chinese cleaver or sharp knife
cutting board
wire mesh strainer
soup ladle
*sealable plastic pouches or ice
    cube trays*

A delicate blending of flavors that can be used as a base in any recipe. Homemade stock is not only delicious but nutritious too. When you have time, prepare a batch and freeze it in pouches or ice cube trays.

1. Place chicken and bones in large saucepot. Add water and bring to a boil. Immediately turn heat to low. Skim off scum and froth.

2. Add gingerroot, scallions, sherry, salt, and pepper. Cover and cook on low for 3 hours.

3. Skim off scum periodically. After 3 hours, turn off heat and let stock cool on stove for 30 minutes. Remove and discard all bones, gingerroot, and scallions.

4. Strain stock through wire mesh strainer and store in a covered container. Refrigerated, the stock is good for at least a week. Frozen, it can be kept for months.

A convenient way to freeze and store soup stock is to measure, label, and store it in air-tight plastic pouches or in ice cube trays. When stock is needed for soup or sauces, use the required amount.

Yield: 7½ cups

Basic Vegetable Stock

A hearty but meatless soup stock that can also double as a soup by itself. A touch of sugar brings out the natural sweetness of fresh vegetables. When you have time, prepare a batch and freeze it in air-tight plastic pouches or in ice cube trays.

Before you start

Mix seasoning ingredients in cup or small bowl and set aside.

1. Cut onions in half. Slice with the grain into ½-inch wide slices. Place on tray and set aside. If using leeks, discard roots and wash thoroughly. Cut into 1-inch sections and set aside on tray.

2. Wash, pare, and thin-slice carrots. Place on tray and set aside.

3. Cut cabbage in half and slice into ½-inch pieces. Wash celery ribs and cut into ½-inch pieces. Wash radishes and cut off ends. Cut each radish in half. Place cut vegetables on tray and set aside.

4. With the flat side of a Chinese cleaver or knife, smash gingerroot slices.

5. Place water in saucepot, add gingerroot and onion slices, cover, and bring to boil.

6. Add all other vegetables. Continue cooking on high until stock comes to a second boil.

7. Skim off foam. Add seasoning ingredients. Turn heat to medium low. Cover and simmer for 2 hours.

8. After 2 hours, turn off heat and let cool on stove for 30 minutes. Remove and discard all vegetables. Strain stock through wire mesh strainer and store in covered container. Refrigerated, the stock is good for at least a week. Frozen, it can be kept for months.

Yield: 8 cups

Seasoning

1 teaspoon salt
¼ teaspoon white pepper
1 teaspoon sugar
2 tablespoons dry sherry, gin, or vodka, optional

Ingredients

2 large onions or 2 leeks
4 large carrots
1 small head cabbage, about 1 pound
6 celery ribs
1 bunch red radishes
4 slices gingerroot, each about (TS) size of a 50-cent piece
12 cups cold water

Equipment

measuring spoons and cups
large spoon
cup or small bowl
6- or 8-quart saucepot with lid
Chinese cleaver or sharp knife
cutting board
wire mesh strainer
tray for ingredients
soup ladle
sealable plastic pouches or ice cube trays

Roast Pork
(Chinese Barbecued Pork or Char Siu)

———— ◆ ————

Marinade

½ teaspoon five-spice powder
½ teaspoon black pepper
½ cup hoisin sauce
¼ cup soy sauce
1 tablespoon oyster sauce
(S) ½ cup chicken soup stock, freshly
    made (p. 22) or ½ cup canned
    chicken broth
¼ cup honey
2 tablespoons dry sherry, gin, or
    vodka, optional

Ingredients

2 pounds lean pork, preferably
    boneless butt or rolled roast

Equipment

measuring spoons and cups
large spoon
large bowl or container with lid
9 x 13-inch baking pan
heavy-duty aluminum foil
Chinese cleaver or sharp knife
cutting board
pastry brush
timer
jar with lid
serving platter

Roast pork, Chinese barbecued pork, or Char Siu, as the Cantonese call it, ranks among the traditional favorites of the Chinese. It is still a standard item sold in a Chinese barbecue shop. Because many Chinese homes do not have a conventional oven, it is easier to buy a pound or more at the store and use it ready made. The taste marries well with many ingredients, but roast pork can also be eaten alone as an appetizer. Once you have learned the technique of making roast pork, you can combine it with almost anything.

Before you start
Preheat oven at 375° for 5 minutes.

1. Cut pork into 2 x 2 x 5-inch strips.

2. Mix marinade ingredients together in large bowl until smooth. Add pork strips. Marinate meat in refrigerator for at least 3 hours or overnight in a covered container. Marinating longer will enhance the flavor of the pork. Turn and baste meat several times.

3. Line baking pan with double layers of aluminum foil to make cleanup easier. Spread pork strips evenly in pan and pour marinade over the pork. Roast pork uncovered, in middle of oven at 375° for 30 minutes. Turn the strips, baste, and roast for 30 minutes longer, until the pork is browned but not burned.

4. Remove meat to platter, and let cool for about 15 minutes.

5. Slice strips diagonally into thin slices (p. 20). If roast pork is made ahead of time, do not slice until ready to serve. Roast pork can be stored in refrigerator without loss of flavor for at least a week.

6. To make more gravy, add 1 cup chicken broth to residue in pan. Mix well. Skim off fat from gravy. Pour gravy into jar with lid and store in refrigerator. The gravy can be kept for at least a month. It goes well as a sauce over plain rice or noodles. Discard the coagulated fat from sauce before using.

Serve pork slices with warmed gravy. As an appetizer, roast pork can be cut into ½-inch cubes and served with toothpicks. As an entree, it can be thin-sliced and arranged in overlapping layers on a platter, garnished with sprigs of watercress or parsley.

Note

Delicious served warm or cold. Can be used in salads, sandwiches, or as filling for pita bread. Recipe can be doubled or quadrupled. Roast pork can be easily warmed up with gravy in microwave.

Yield: 6 or more servings

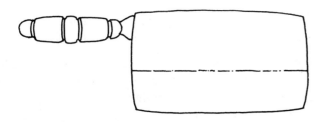

No-work Chicken

Seasoning

½ teaspoon white pepper
½ teaspoon sugar
2 tablespoons dry sherry, gin, or
vodka, optional

Ingredients

(S) *6 cups freshly made chicken*
soup stock (p. 22) or
1 can (48-ounces) chicken broth
6 cups cold water
2 scallions with green tops,
washed and with roots
removed, but kept whole
3 slices fresh gingerroot, each
about size of a 50-cent piece,
smashed with a cleaver or
heavy knife
1 3-pound fryer, washed, with
innards and all fat removed
2 tablespoons sesame seed oil

Believe it or not, this chicken requires no work, for it cooks itself without supervision. If this sounds too easy to be true, you have a pleasant surprise in store for you. Chicken cooked this way is not only tender, but it can be served in dozens of ways, combined with different ingredients. Taste it and see . . .

Before you start

Mix seasoning ingredients in cup or small bowl and set aside.

1. Place chicken stock in saucepot large enough to hold entire fryer comfortably. Add 6 cups water. Add scallions, gingerroot, and seasonings. Bring stock to a rolling boil.

2. Put chicken, breast-side down, in boiling broth, which should cover chicken completely. If needed, add another cup boiling water to cover chicken completely. Cover pot with tight-fitting lid and bring to a boil. Continue to boil on high for 5 minutes. If you like your chicken well cooked, boil for 3 to 5 minutes longer.

3. Turn off heat and remove pot from stove. DO NOT LIFT LID AT ALL. Chicken should remain in pot until it cools to room temperature, about 5 to 6 hours, or overnight. Since the lid was on when the stock was boiling, the flavor is sealed and the contents, not exposed to outside air, are germ-free. To remind myself and others not to peek, I usually place 2 heavy-duty rubber bands over the knob in the middle of the lid and stretch to secure them to the handles.

4. When the sides of the pot are cool to the touch, remove the chicken and pat dry with paper towels. Brush chicken with sesame seed oil, using a pastry brush. Place chicken in a large bowl and cover with plastic wrap or lid. Refrigerate until ready to use.

5. Discard scallions and gingerroot. Strain and refrigerate broth to use later in soups. If preferred, after fat has been skimmed off, measure and pour broth into sealable plastic pouches or ice cube trays to store in freezer.

6. Slice the chicken as an entree and serve it with a dip* or use it in different recipes, see pp. 65–70. It is also delicious when served together with Crunchy Noodle Salad (p. 90).

*Oyster Sauce-Sesame Dip

Mix 4 tablespoons oyster sauce, 2 tablespoons sesame seed oil, and 2 tablespoons warm water in small bowl. Blend well. Spoon sauce over sliced chicken.

*Sizzling Dip

Fine-slice 3 scallions and 4 thin slices of fresh gingerroot. Place in small heat-proof bowl. Add 1 teaspoon salt. In small saucepot, heat 6 tablespoons corn, vegetable, or safflower oil for 5 minutes, to about 350°, just below boiling point. Pour hot oil over scallion-ginger mixture and listen to the sizzling sound. Spoon sizzling dip over chicken.

Note

For health and safety sake, it is important that you DO NOT lift the lid at all until the chicken is cooked, then refrigerate the chicken and stock separately. If your saucepot does not have a tight-fitting lid, use double layers of heavy-duty aluminum foil between the lid and the top of the saucepot to seal the steam.

Yield: 6 to 8 servings

Equipment

measuring spoons and cups
large spoon
cup or small bowl
small bowls for dips
4-quart heavy saucepot with
   tight-fitting lid
Chinese cleaver or sharp knife
cutting board
pastry brush
strainer
2 heavy-duty rubber bands
paper towels
plastic wrap
sealable plastic pouches or ice
   cube trays
serving platter

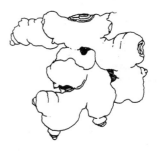

Mandarin Roast Duck

Marinade

¼ cup soy sauce

¼ cup vodka or gin

Ingredients

1 frozen duckling, about 4½
    pounds, thoroughly defrosted

2 scallions with green tops,
    washed, with roots discarded
    but left whole

(TS) 10 to 12 fried shrimp chips (p. 18)

1 cup Instant Sweet and Sour
    Sauce (p. 116), optional

Equipment

measuring cups
cup or small bowl
bowls for sauces
large spoon
11 x 17-inch baking pan with rack
Chinese cleaver or sharp knife
cutting board
kitchen shears
colander or strainer
pastry brush
large tongs
timer
heavy-duty aluminum foil
paper towels
container or plastic box with lid
    (large enough to hold duck
    comfortably)
serving platter

Here is a duck that rivals any served in the best Chinese restaurants. It's tender, succulent, and soooo easy to prepare. After marinating overnight in liquor and soy sauce, the duck is slowly roasted to a golden brown. Try it, then believe . . . and enjoy!

Before you start

Mix marinade ingredients in cup or small bowl and set aside.

1. Remove neck and innards from duck cavity and save to use later in soup stock. Remove fat from neck and tail area. Cut off flap of skin from neck. Rinse duck well under cold running water. Drain and pat dry gently and thoroughly with paper towels. Take care not to break or tear the skin.

2. Place duck in container or plastic box. Pour marinade over duck. With pastry brush, spread marinade evenly on both sides of duck. Cover the container and refrigerate. Marinate duck overnight, turning occasionally.

3. When ready to prepare the next day, preheat oven to 325° for 10 minutes.

4. Tuck scallions into the cavity of duck. Place duck, breast side up, on rack in roasting pan lined with double layers of aluminum foil in middle of oven. Roast duck, uncovered, for 1 hour, basting with leftover marinade at least every 15 minutes.

5. Turn duck and roast on the other side for 1 hour. Baste at least every 15 minutes with marinade. Continue basting until all marinade is used.

6. Remove duck to platter. Garnish with shrimp chips (p. 18). Slice duck and serve plain or with sweet and sour sauce.

Note

The traditional method of preparing roast duck is an elaborate procedure that requires many steps and much preparation. I have simplified the technique, but it still requires advance planning. Roast duck can be stored in the refrigerator and the meat served in salads, such as Chinese Coleslaw (p. 88), Chinese Gourmet Salad (p. 91), or as a garnish for Noodles in Soup (p. 108). The carcass can be stored in the freezer to be used for soup stock later.

Yield: 4 to 6 servings

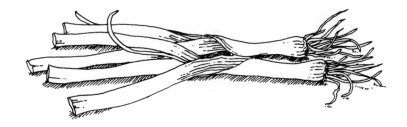

Tea Eggs

Ingredients

6 eggs
4 cups cold water, divided
2 bags of oolong or red tea

Seasoning

1 teaspoon sugar
½ teaspoon salt
½ teaspoon black pepper
½ teaspoon five-spice powder
3 tablespoons soy sauce
1 tablespoon sesame seed oil
1 tablespoon dry sherry, gin, or
   vodka, optional

Equipment

measuring spoons and cups
large spoon
1½-quart saucepot with lid
Chinese cleaver or sharp knife
cutting board
small knife
covered container
serving plate

Eggs with a flourish! Exciting to look at, even more exciting to eat, by itself or in combination with a salad or an item on an appetizer tray. Also great as a garnish.

1. Place eggs in saucepot and cover with 2 cups cold water. Bring water to slow boil. When water boils, reduce heat, cover, and simmer for 15 minutes.

2. Turn off heat and let eggs cool in hot water for 30 minutes, then drain. Add cold water to cover and let sit for 10 minutes. DO NOT PEEL SHELLS. Tap eggs gently with back of small knife so that the entire shell cracks in a fine pattern. Return eggs with cracked shells to saucepot. Add 2 cups cold water to cover.

3. Mix seasoning ingredients together in cup or small bowl. Add to eggs in saucepot, together with tea bags. Bring to boil over high heat. Reduce heat, cover, and let eggs simmer for 1 hour. Let eggs sit, covered, in saucepot at room temperature until cooled, about 3 to 4 hours or overnight. Transfer eggs and sauce to covered container and refrigerate for at least 2 hours before peeling.

4. Peel shells carefully. The white will be laced with dark marbelized lines.

5. Cut eggs in halves or quarters to serve.

Note

This recipe can easily be doubled. Tea Eggs can be made ahead of time and stored in a covered container in the refrigerator for at least a week.

Yield: 4 to 6 servings

Pickled Spicy Cabbage

A simple and not too spicy salad with the zest of hot pepper and garlic. It can be served as a side dish to perk up mild entrees.

Before you start

Place seasoning ingredients in 4-quart jar or container and blend well. Set aside.

1. Peel off outer leaves of cabbage and discard. Cut cabbage in half, then quarter. Core and discard. Cut each quarter into 2 wedges, then into 2 x 2-inch pieces.

2. Using kitchen gloves, cut dry peppers into halves or quarters. Add to seasoning ingredients.

3. Add cold water to jar and mix well. Add cabbage. With clean chopsticks or wooden spoon, stir well and cover cabbage with seasoning. Cover tightly and refrigerate for at least 24 hours.

Each time you serve, you must use a clean fork or spoon. Pickled cabbage can be stored, refrigerated, in a covered jar or container for several months.

Note

This recipe is simple to prepare and not too spicy hot. If you prefer a hotter flavor, double the amount of red peppers and peppercorns. While the salad is ready for the table after 24 hours, longer refrigeration will enhance the flavor. After the cabbage is eaten, the pickling juice can be reused by adding more hot peppers, peppercorns, and the other seasonings. Sample the pickling juice for best results.

Yield: 8 to 12 servings

Seasoning

1 cup sugar
2 tablespoons dry peppercorns
1 teaspoon salt
2 cups cider vinegar
4 tablespoons diced fresh scallions (TS) or 2 scallions with green tops, diced
2 teaspoons minced fresh garlic or (TS) 4 large cloves garlic, finely minced

Ingredients

1 head cabbage, about 2 pounds
20 dried small hot red peppers
1½ quarts cold water

Equipment

measuring spoons and cups
wooden spoon or chopsticks
Chinese cleaver or sharp knife
cutting board
tray for ingredients
4-quart jar or plastic container with tight-fitting lid
kitchen gloves

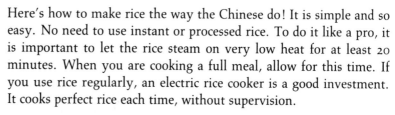

Steamed Rice

Ingredients
1 cup long grain white rice
1½ cups cold water

Equipment
measuring cups
1½-quart saucepot with lid
chopsticks or fork
serving bowl

Here's how to make rice the way the Chinese do! It is simple and so easy. No need to use instant or processed rice. To do it like a pro, it is important to let the rice steam on very low heat for at least 20 minutes. When you are cooking a full meal, allow for this time. If you use rice regularly, an electric rice cooker is a good investment. It cooks perfect rice each time, without supervision.

1. Put rice in saucepot and rinse twice with cold water. Pour off excess water by cupping hand over rice grains.

2. Add cold water to rice in saucepot and bring to boil over high heat.

3. When water bubbles to top of saucepot in about 6 minutes, turn heat to moderate and continue cooking. Stir with chopsticks or fork occasionally to prevent rice from sticking to the pot.

4. After water has evaporated, in about 3 minutes, turn heat to simmer. Cover with a tight-fitting lid and steam for at least 20 minutes. Do not lift cover.

5. After steaming is complete, uncover. Fluff rice with chopsticks or fork. Replace lid and let stand until ready to serve.

Note

When doubling or quadrupling this recipe, use the following formula: 2 cups of rice to 2½ cups of water; 3 cups of rice to 3¾ cups of water. Remember to rinse the rice twice and use larger saucepots for larger quantities. Day-old rice is ideal for fried rice dishes. Plan ahead. Cook a large pot of rice when you have the time, store in the refrigerator in a covered container and you will have enough to make fried rice for a week.

Yield: 3½ cups

Almond Cookies

These cookies—tasty and light—are better than any served in Chinese restaurants. The secret? Ground almonds, of course! They are also excellent tea cookies.

1. Mix flour, baking soda, and salt together into medium bowl and set aside.

2. Cream shortening and sugar in large mixing bowl in electric mixer until smooth. Add eggs, one at a time, and blend together thoroughly. Add almond extract.

3. Add dry ingredients gradually and mix well. Blend the ingredients together thoroughly until a firm, smooth dough is formed.

4. Add ground almonds and blend into batter well with mixer or by hand with wooden spoon.

5. Chill dough in covered bowl for 4 hours or overnight.

6. Cut dough into 4 parts. Shape each part into a cylinder about 1-inch in diameter. With sharp knife, cut each length of dough crosswise into 1-inch sections. Roll these sections into 1-inch balls and place them about an inch apart on ungreased cookie sheets.

7. Press one almond half into center of each cookie, to flatten cookie slightly.

8. Bake for 10 to 12 minutes in preheated 350° oven.

9. Remove cookies from oven and cool on baking rack. Store in cookie jar or covered tin.

Note

These cookies can be made ahead of time and stored in a cookie jar or tin for up to several weeks.

Yield: 5 to 6 dozen

Ingredients

2½ cups all-purpose flour, unsifted
½ teaspoon baking soda
½ teaspoon salt
1 cup lard or vegetable shortening
1 cup sugar
3 eggs
2 tablespoons almond extract
½ cup ground almonds
1 cup blanched almond halves

Equipment

measuring spoons and cups
large mixing spoons
wooden spoon
medium bowl
large bowl
electric mixer
ungreased cookie sheets
baking rack
sharp knife
cutting board or pastry cloth

Shrimp Chips

◆

Ingredients

3 cups corn, vegetable, or
   safflower oil
2 cups (¼-pound) dried shrimp
   chips (or prawn crackers)

Equipment

deep-fryer or 4-quart saucepot
11 x 17-inch baking pan
wire mesh strainer
paper towels

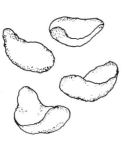

Chinese shrimp chips are thin white or pastel-colored dried dough made from flour and a touch of shrimp or lobster. When deep-fried, they are cooked within seconds, so you have to work very fast. They are quite different from potato chips but just as tasty. See if you can stop at just one!

1. Line baking pan with double layers of paper towels.

2. Heat oil in deep fryer or saucepot until very hot, about 375°. When oil is almost smoking, drop in a handful of dried shrimp chips.

3. Within 5 seconds, the chips will unfurl and triple in size. Remove immediately with wire mesh strainer. Drain on paper towels in pan.

   Serve as a snack or with cocktails. Also excellent as a garnish for dishes like Mandarin Roast Duck (p. 28) or No-work Chicken (p. 26).

Note

Fried chips can be stored in a tightly-covered can or plastic bag for a few days without losing their crunchiness. Store unused portion in tightly-sealed plastic bags. A package (½-pound) contains about 4 cups of dried chips. Each cup has about 50 chips.

Yield: 5 servings (100 chips)

Beef on a Stick

It's robust, it's great as an appetizer or an entree, and it's very Chinese. This recipe is easy to prepare ahead of time, then cook in the oven just before guests arrive.

Before you start

Preheat oven to broil. Mix marinade ingredients together in medium bowl.

1. Add beef slices to marinade in medium bowl and turn to coat meat evenly. Let stand at least 5 minutes. Marinating longer will enhance the flavor of the beef.

2. Line baking sheet with double layers of aluminum foil to make cleanup easier.

3. Weave a skewer like a needle through the center of each slice of beef. Place each skewer side by side on the lined baking sheet. With rubber spatula, spread remaining marinade over beef.

4. Broil beef strips on bottom rack of oven farthest from heat for 2½ minutes. Turn skewers and broil for 2½ minutes longer. If you like your meat well done, broil each side for 1 minute longer.

Transfer skewers to serving platter to serve.

Variation

A tablespoon of Hunan chili paste or any brand of Chinese chili paste can be substituted for oyster sauce. Different brands vary in intensity of hotness. Experiment for best results.

Yield: 10 to 12 skewers

Marinade

1 teaspoon cornstarch
½ teaspoon sugar
¼ teaspoon black pepper
¼ teaspoon baking soda
1 tablespoon soy sauce
1 tablespoon oyster sauce or Worcestershire sauce
1 teaspoon sesame seed oil
1 teaspoon minced fresh garlic or (TS) 2 large cloves garlic, finely minced
½ tablespoon dry sherry, gin, or vodka, optional

Ingredients

½ pound flank, round, or sirloin steak, well-trimmed of all fat, sliced ¼-inch thick x 5-inches long

Equipment

measuring spoons
large spoon
medium bowl
11 x 17-inch baking sheet
Chinese cleaver or sharp knife
cutting board
rubber spatula
tongs
10 to 12 8-inch bamboo skewers
heavy-duty aluminum foil
serving platter

Shrimp Toast

◆

Seasoning

2 teaspoons cornstarch
½ teaspoon salt
½ teaspoon sugar
⅛ teaspoon white pepper
1 egg white
(TS) ½ teaspoon minced fresh garlic or
1 large clove garlic, minced
(TS) 2 tablespoons fresh scallions or 1
scallion with green top, diced

Ingredients

¼ pound fresh or frozen shrimp,
shelled, deveined, and uncooked
5 canned whole water chestnuts
½ small carrot, cut into chunks
6 slices thin, firm white or rye
bread, at least a day old*
3 cups corn, vegetable, or
safflower oil

Equipment

measuring spoons and cups
large spoon, medium bowl
food processor, Chinese cleaver
deep-fryer or 4-quart saucepot
cutting board, small knife
colander, tray for ingredients
tongs or Chinese wire strainer
paring knife or peeler
paper towels, serving platter

*Use firm, dry bread that will absorb
little oil.

This tasty appetizer, which takes only minutes to make, comes to the table hot, golden, and delicious. No wonder it is in demand by Chinese gourmets all over the world.

Before you start

Mix seasoning ingredients together in medium bowl until smooth.

1. Wash and drain shrimp. Place shrimp, water chestnuts, carrot, and seasoning in food processor and fine-chop until a paste is formed. Transfer contents to medium bowl.

2. Quarter each slice of bread into 4 squares or triangles. Trim crusts, if you prefer.

3. Heat oil in deep fryer or saucepot until smoking, about 375°. This will take about 4 to 5 minutes. If the oil gets too hot before the shrimp toasts are ready to be fried, turn heat to medium.

4. Spread shrimp mixture generously on bread pieces with small knife until all spread is used.

5. Fry toast in very hot oil, spread side down, for about 1 minute, until golden brown, but not burned. Turn and fry on the other side for 30 seconds. Remove with tongs. Drain on paper towels.

Serve hot.

Note

The recipe can easily be doubled or quadrupled. Shrimp toast can also be made ahead of time and reheated for about 8 minutes in a 250° oven.

Yield: 4 to 6 servings (24 pieces)

Sesame Pork Balls

An exciting new way of making meatballs to serve to family and friends. Your guests will long remember this dish: very Chinese, very different, and unforgettably delicious.

Before you start

Mix marinade ingredients together in medium bowl until smooth. Spread sesame seeds evenly on a large plate.

1. Add ground pork to marinade in bowl. Blend thoroughly.

2. Heat oil in deep-fryer until smoking, about 375°. If the oil gets too hot before the sesame balls are ready to be fried, turn heat to medium.

3. For each meatball, scoop out 1 heaping teaspoon of pork mixture. Wet your hands and shape into a ball. Place on plate with sesame seeds. Continue until all meat is used.

4. Roll each meatball in sesame seeds until it is completely covered with sesame seeds. Lower sesame balls gently into hot oil and deep-fry for about 3 minutes, until crisp and golden but not burned.

   Serve hot with litchi sauce.

Note

Sesame Pork Balls can be made ahead of time and fried at the last minute.

Yield: 4 servings (about 25 sesame pork balls)

Marinade

1 tablespoon cornstarch
½ tablespoon dried onion flakes
¼ teaspoon salt
⅛ teaspoon black pepper
1 tablespoon soy sauce
½ tablespoon oyster sauce
½ teaspoon sesame seed oil
½ tablespoon cold water
½ tablespoon dry sherry, gin, or vodka, optional

Ingredients

⅓ cup untoasted sesame seeds
½ pound lean ground pork
3 cups corn, vegetable, or safflower oil
1 cup Instant Litchi Sauce (p. 116)

Equipment

measuring spoons and cups
large spoon
medium bowl
large plate
deep-fryer or 4-quart deep saucepot
serving platter

Golden Wontons

Ingredients

4 to 6 leaves from head or leaf
lettuce, washed and drained

(TS) 2 fresh shiitake mushrooms or 2
medium presoaked Chinese
black mushrooms (p. 9), or 2
large fresh mushrooms

¼ cup lean ground pork or beef

16 wonton wrappers, ready-made
(available from the
supermarket)

3 cups corn, vegetable, or
safflower oil

½ cup Instant Litchi Sauce
(p. 116) Instant Sweet and
Sour Sauce (p. 116), or wine
vinegar for dipping

Seasoning

2 teaspoons cornstarch

¼ teaspoon sugar

dash of black pepper

1 teaspoon soy sauce

1 teaspoon oyster sauce

1 teaspoon cold water

½ teaspoon sesame seed oil

(TS) 2 tablespoons diced fresh scallions
or 1 scallion with green top,
diced

(TS) ½ teaspoon minced fresh garlic or
1 large clove garlic, finely
minced

1 teaspoon dry sherry, gin, or
vodka, optional

Light as clouds (the literal translation of wonton) and delicious. Dipped in litchi sauce or sweet and sour sauce, they are irresistible. Try them and see if you can eat just one!

Before you start

Mix seasoning ingredients in cup or small bowl until smooth. Arrange lettuce leaves on platter.

1. Wash fresh shiitake mushrooms. Cut off and discard stems. If using presoaked Chinese black mushrooms, squeeze dry. Cut off and discard stems. If using fresh mushrooms, wash and set aside.

2. Place mushrooms, ground pork, and seasoning in food processor and fine-chop. Transfer contents to medium bowl. Set aside.

3. Place a wonton wrapper on a small plate. Place about 1 teaspoon of meat mixture in center of a wonton wrapper.

4. Dip your fingers in cold water and moisten edges of wrapper. Fold wrapper into a triangle. Twist both ends to a point. Pinch and seal with water. You now have a wonton, ready to deep-fry.

5. Heat oil in deep-fryer or saucepot until smoking, about 375°. This will take about 4 to 5 minutes. If the oil gets too hot before the wontons are ready to be fried, turn heat to medium.

6. Continue wrapping wontons until all wrappers are used. Place on a plate lined with wax paper.

7. Drop wontons into hot oil one by one. Deep-fry wontons for 2 minutes, or until crisp and golden but not burned.

8. Remove wontons from saucepot with tongs and drain on paper towels.

Place fried wontons on a platter lined with lettuce leaves and serve hot with litchi sauce, sweet and sour sauce, or wine vinegar.

Note

This recipe can easily be doubled or quadrupled. Wontons can be made ahead of time and deep-fried. They can be reheated in a 350° oven for 10 to 12 minutes before serving. Wontons can also be wrapped and frozen, uncooked, in a covered container and kept in the freezer for at least a month. They must be thoroughly defrosted before they can be deep-fried.

Yield: 2 to 4 servings (16 wontons)

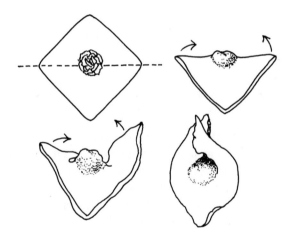

Equipment

measuring spoons and cups
large spoon
cup or small bowl
small bowl with cold water for dipping fingers
medium bowl
small plate
large plate
food processor
deep-fryer or 4-quart saucepot
Chinese cleaver or sharp knife
cutting board
tongs or Chinese wire strainer
wax paper
paper towels
serving platter

Quickie Egg Rolls

◈

Marinade

1 tablespoon cornstarch
¼ teaspoon sugar
⅛ teaspoon black pepper
1 teaspoon soy sauce
1 teaspoon oyster sauce
(TS) 2 tablespoons fresh scallions or 1
scallion with green top, diced
(TS) ½ teaspoon minced fresh garlic or
1 large clove garlic, finely
minced
1 teaspoon dry sherry, gin, or
vodka, optional

Ingredients

¼ cup lean ground pork
4 to 6 leaves from head or leaf
lettuce, washed and drained
1 cup fresh bean sprouts
3 cups corn, vegetable, or
safflower oil
4 egg roll wrappers, ready-made
(available from the
supermarket)
½ cup Instant Litchi Sauce
(p. 116), Instant Sweet and
Sour Sauce (p. 116), or wine
vinegar

Equipment

measuring spoons and cups
large spoon
small bowl
small bowl filled with cold water
bowl for dipping sauce

A quick recipe for an all-time favorite. Even the pickiest eater will find these hard to resist.

Before you start

Mix marinade ingredients together in small bowl until smooth. Add pork to marinade and blend well. Arrange lettuce leaves on platter.

1. Wash and drain bean sprouts. Divide into 4 portions and set aside.

2. Heat oil in deep-fryer or saucepot until it is very hot, about 375°. This will take about 4 to 5 minutes. If the oil gets too hot before the egg rolls are ready to be fried, turn heat to medium.

3. Place an egg roll wrapper on a clean plate. Place one portion of bean sprouts diagonally across the lower section of a wrapper. Top with one tablespoon of marinated meat spread evenly across top of bean sprouts.

4. Bring the tip of the corner square over the filling and roll once. Bring left and right flaps together to make an envelope and wet tips to seal. Continue rolling to form a neat, tight roll. Seal the last tip with water. The roll should be sealed very tightly so the filling will stay intact, and the roll will not unravel when it is fried. You now have a 4-inch egg roll.

5. Make the other 3 egg rolls in the same way.

6. Gently place the egg rolls side by side in very hot oil and deep-fry until golden brown, but not burned, about 3 to 4 minutes.

Place deep-fried egg rolls on a platter lined with lettuce leaves and serve hot with litchi sauce, sweet and sour sauce, or wine vinegar.

This recipe can easily be doubled or quadrupled. Egg rolls can be made ahead of time and deep-fried. They can be reheated in a 350° oven for 15 minutes before serving.

Yield: 2 to 4 servings (4 egg rolls)

dinner plate
deep-fryer or 4-quart saucepot
Chinese cleaver or sharp knife
cutting board
colander or strainer
tongs or Chinese wire strainer
serving platter

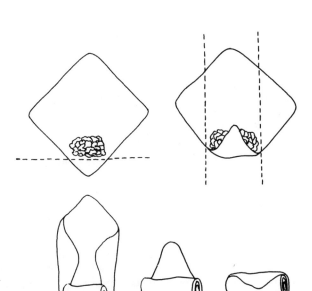

Vegetarian Egg Rolls

Vegetarians don't have to feel neglected. These egg rolls have an all-vegetable filling.

Seasoning

1 tablespoon cornstarch
½ teaspoon sugar
½ teaspoon salt
⅛ teaspoon black pepper
½ tablespoon soy sauce
(TS) 2 tablespoons fresh scallions or 1 scallion with green top, diced
(TS) ½ teaspoon minced fresh garlic or 1 large clove garlic, finely minced
1 teaspoon dry sherry, gin, or vodka, optional

Ingredients

(TS) ¼ cup presoaked crunchy mushrooms (won yee or cloud ears) or 1 tablespoon dried crunchy mushrooms
1 cup boiling water
4 to 6 leaves from head or leaf lettuce, washed and drained
½ cup fresh bean sprouts
3 cups corn, vegetable, or safflower oil
½ cup frozen french cut green beans, well-thawed
4 egg roll wrappers, ready-made (from the supermarket)
½ cup Instant Litchi Sauce (p. 116), Instant Sweet and Sour Sauce (p. 116), or wine vinegar

Before you start

Mix seasoning ingredients together in large bowl until smooth. Soak dried crunchy mushrooms in 1 cup boiling water for 3 minutes. Arrange lettuce leaves on serving platter.

1. Wash and drain bean sprouts. Set aside.

2. Heat oil in deep-fryer or saucepot until it is very hot, about 375°. This will take about 4 to 5 minutes. If the oil gets too hot before the egg rolls are ready to be fried, turn heat to medium.

3. When the crunchy mushrooms are soft and have expanded to 4 times their original size, squeeze dry. Remove hard particles and shred finely with Chinese cleaver or sharp knife. Set aside.

4. Add mushrooms, bean sprouts, and green beans to seasoning ingredients in large bowl. Toss to blend well. Drain in colander to remove excess juice. Divide vegetables into 4 portions.

5. Place an egg roll wrapper on a clean plate. Place one portion (about ¼ cup) of vegetable mixture diagonally across the lower section of a wrapper. Bring the tip of the corner square over the filling and roll once. Bring left and right flaps together to make an envelope and wet each tip to seal. Continue rolling to form a neat tight roll. Seal the last tip with water. The roll should be sealed very tightly so the filling will stay intact and the roll will not unravel when it is fried. You now have a 4-inch egg roll. (See diagrams on p. 41)

6. Make the other 3 egg rolls in the same way.

7. Gently place the egg rolls side by side in oil and deep-fry until golden brown, but not burned, about 3 minutes.

Place fried egg rolls on a platter lined with lettuce leaves and serve hot with litchi sauce, sweet and sour sauce, or wine vinegar.

Note

This recipe can easily be doubled or quadrupled. Egg rolls can be made ahead of time and deep-fried. They can be reheated in a 350° oven for 15 minutes before serving.

Yield: 2 to 4 servings (4 egg rolls)

Equipment

measuring spoons and cups
large spoon
small bowl with cold water for
   dipping fingers
bowl for dipping sauce
large bowl
dinner plate
2-quart saucepot
deep-fryer or 4-quart saucepot
Chinese cleaver or sharp knife
cutting board
colander or strainer
tongs or Chinese wire strainer
serving platter

Lettuce Rolls

Egg rolls of the 21st century! Crunchy lettuce leaves hide full-flavored meat and filling. Diners can enjoy to their heart's delight and get their fiber and protein too.

Marinade

½ teaspoon cornstarch
½ teaspoon sugar
⅛ teaspoon baking soda
⅛ teaspoon black pepper
1 teaspoon soy sauce
1 teaspoon oyster sauce
1 teaspoon cold water
½ teaspoon sesame seed oil
1 teaspoon dry sherry, gin, or vodka, optional

Ingredients

¼ cup hoisin sauce
¼ cup oyster sauce
¼ cup lean ground chuck or lean ground pork
4 large whole leaves from head or leaf lettuce
ice cubes and water
(TS) 4 fresh shiitake mushrooms or 4 small presoaked Chinese dried black mushrooms (p. 16)
8 water chestnuts
1 tablespoon corn, vegetable, or safflower oil
¼ cup frozen green peas, well-thawed
¼ teaspoon salt
⅛ teaspoon black pepper

Equipment

measuring spoons and cups
large spoon or spatula
3 small and 1 medium bowl

Before you start

Mix marinade ingredients together in small bowl and set aside. Place hoisin sauce and oyster sauce in separate small bowls and set aside.

1. Add ground meat to marinade in bowl and blend well. Set aside.

2. Soak lettuce leaves in large bowl filled with ice cubes and water. Set aside.

3. Wash fresh shiitake mushrooms. Cut off and discard stems. Place mushrooms and water chestnuts in food processor. Fine-mince and set aside.

4. Heat skillet or wok on high for 30 seconds. Add oil to coat skillet for 30 seconds longer. Add mushrooms, water chestnuts, and peas. Stir-toss and blend well for 1 minute. Add salt and black pepper and mix again. Add marinated beef and stir-toss for 2 minutes, until meat loses its pink color. Remove to serving platter.

5. Drain lettuce leaves and place on separate platter.

Diners wrap their own lettuce roll. Place a leaf on a plate, spread a little hoisin or oyster sauce, then spoon ¼ of beef mixture onto the leaf. Roll, wrap, and enjoy!

Note

This recipe can easily be doubled or quadrupled. The filling can be cooked ahead of time and reheated just before serving. Lettuce leaves can be crisped a day ahead and refrigerated in a covered container.

Yield: 2 to 4 servings (4 lettuce rolls)

large bowl
food processor
10-inch skillet or 14-inch wok
Chinese cleaver or sharp knife
cutting board
colander or strainer
tray for ingredients
2 serving platters

Cucumber Soup

◆

Ingredients

(S) *4 cups chicken soup stock, freshly made (p. 22), or 4 cups canned chicken broth*
1 large cucumber
2 ounces boiled ham slices
(TS) *2 tablespoons diced fresh scallions or 1 scallion with green top, diced*
salt and white pepper to taste

Equipment

measuring spoons and cups
large spoon or chopsticks
2-quart saucepot with lid
paring knife or peeler
Chinese cleaver or sharp knife
cutting board
soup ladle
4 soup bowls

Cool, delicate, and different, this colorful soup will delight your palate. Soup lovers take note!

1. Bring soup stock to boil in covered saucepot.

2. While stock is boiling, pare and cut off both ends of cucumber. Cut into half crosswise, then half lengthwise. Cut each quarter diagonally into ¼-inch thick pieces (p. 20).

3. Stack ham slices, then cut in half. Stack halves again and slice into ½ x 1-inch wide pieces. Set aside.

4. When stock comes to a boil, add cucumber slices, cover, and cook over moderate heat for 3 minutes. Add ham slices and cook for 30 seconds longer.

5. Remove from heat. Add diced scallions and salt and pepper to taste.

   Ladle to soup bowls and serve.

Variation

For a vegetarian soup, use freshly made vegetable soup stock (p. 23). Substitute ½ cup sliced mushrooms or tofu cubes for the ham.

Yield: 4 servings

Tofu with Spinach Soup

A soup noted for its classic simplicity. Tofu and spinach work well in this appealing combination of light and dark color contrasts.

1. Bring soup stock to boil in covered saucepot.

2. While stock is boiling, rinse fresh spinach leaves, taking care to remove all dirt. Use both stems and leaves for soup. Set aside.

3. Cut tofu into 1 x 1 x ⅛-inch thick slices. Set aside.

4. Add spinach and tofu slices to boiling stock.

5. When soup comes to a second boil, cover, turn heat to medium, and cook for 2 minutes longer.

6. Uncover, add sesame oil, salt, and pepper to taste.

   Ladle to soup bowls and serve.

Variation

For a vegetarian soup, use freshly made vegetable soup stock (p. 23).

Yield: 4 servings

Ingredients

*4 cups chicken soup stock, freshly (S)
    made (p. 22), or 4 cups canned
    chicken broth*
*½ pound fresh spinach, or 1
    (10-ounces) package of frozen
    leaf spinach, thawed*
½ pound firm tofu, drained
1 teaspoon sesame seed oil
salt and pepper to taste

Equipment

measuring spoons and cups
large spoon
2-quart saucepot with lid
colander or strainer
Chinese cleaver or sharp knife
cutting board
soup ladle
4 soup bowls

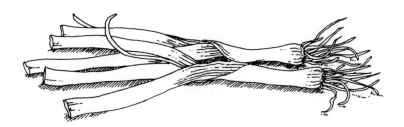

Tomato and Egg Soup

Ingredients

(S) 4 cups chicken soup stock, freshly made (p. 22), or 4 cups canned chicken broth

1 large firm tomato

1 egg, well beaten

(TS) 2 tablespoons diced fresh scallions or 1 scallion with green top, diced

1 teaspoon sesame seed oil

salt and pepper to taste

Equipment

measuring spoons and cups

large spoon

cup or small bowl

2-quart saucepot with lid

Chinese cleaver or sharp knife

cutting board

soup ladle

4 soup bowls

A beautiful soup both to see and eat. The red of the tomato contrasts brightly with the egg and scallions. This soup is tasty all year round, but especially when tomatoes are at their ripest and sweetest.

1. Bring soup stock to boil in covered saucepot.

2. While stock is boiling, wash tomato and cut off front end. Cut tomato in half, then slice thinly into ⅛-inch wedges. Add tomato wedges to boiling soup stock, cover, and continue cooking on moderate high heat for 4 minutes.

3. Turn off heat. Slowly pour in beaten egg and stir gently, until egg is cooked, about 30 seconds. Add diced scallions and sesame seed oil. Add salt and pepper to taste.

Ladle to soup bowls and serve.

Variation

For a vegetarian soup, use freshly made vegetable soup stock (p. 23).

Yield: 4 servings

Floating Blossoms

One of the most dramatic soups in the world. So simple to make and as exciting to serve as it is to eat. From the soft white blossoms to the tasty minced ham, the soup satisfies the appetite and the senses.

Before you start

Chill metal bowl in freezer for 3 minutes.

1. Bring soup stock to boil in covered saucepot.

2. While stock is boiling, fine-mince scallion with Chinese cleaver or sharp knife. Set aside. Fine-mince ham and set aside.

3. Add egg whites and cream of tartar to metal bowl. Beat on high until egg whites are stiff but not dry, about 2 minutes.

4. When stock boils, remove from heat, and spoon egg whites gently onto top of soup with teaspoon. Egg white blossoms should float on surface of soup.

5. Sprinkle scallions and ham over top of egg whites. Add salt and pepper to taste.

   Ladle to soup bowls and serve immediately.

Variation

For a vegetarian soup, use freshly made vegetable soup stock (p. 23) and omit the ham.

Yield: 4 servings

Ingredients

4 cups chicken soup stock, freshly (S) made (p. 22) or 4 cups canned chicken broth
1 scallion with green top
2 very thin slices of cooked ham or prosciutto
2 egg whites
1/4 teaspoon cream of tartar
salt and white pepper to taste

Equipment

measuring spoons and cups
large spoon
small metal bowl
2-quart saucepot with lid
electric mixer
Chinese cleaver or sharp knife
cutting board
soup ladle
4 soup bowls

Wonton Soup

Marinade

2 teaspoons cornstarch

¼ teaspoon sugar

dash of black pepper

1 teaspoon soy sauce

1 teaspoon oyster sauce

1 teaspoon cold water

1 teaspoon dry sherry, gin, or
   vodka, optional

(TS) 2 tablespoons diced fresh scallions
   or 1 scallion with green top, diced

(TS) ½ teaspoon minced fresh garlic or
   1 large clove garlic, finely minced

Ingredients

½ package (10-ounces) frozen leaf
   spinach, thawed

(S) 4 cups homemade chicken stock,
   (p. 22), or 4 cups canned broth

¼ cup lean ground pork or beef

12 wonton wrappers, ready-made
   (available from supermarket)

½ cup cold water

salt and pepper to taste

Equipment

measuring spoons and cups

large spoon, cup or small bowl

small bowl with cold water for
   dipping fingers

small plate, large plate

4-quart saucepot with lid

Chinese cleaver or sharp knife

cutting board, wax paper

soup ladle, 4 soup bowls

A popular soup served in Chinese restaurants. It is as easy to make as it is tasty.

Before you start

Mix marinade ingredients in small bowl until smooth.

1. Add spinach to soup stock and bring to boil in covered saucepot. If wontons are not ready, turn heat to simmer.

2. Add meat to marinade in bowl and mix together well.

3. Place a wonton wrapper on a small plate. Place 1 teaspoon of meat mixture in center of a wonton wrapper.

4. Dip your fingers in cold water and moisten edges of wrapper. Fold wrapper into a triangle. Twist both ends to a point. Pinch and seal with water. You now have a wonton. (See diagrams on p. 39). Continue wrapping wontons until all 12 wrappers are used. Place wontons on a plate lined with wax paper.

5. When soup is boiling, drop wontons into soup one by one. When it comes to a second boil, add ½ cup cold water. Cover, turn heat to low, and cook for 3 minutes longer.

6. Uncover, add salt and pepper to taste.

Ladle to soup bowls and serve.

Yield: 4 to 6 servings

Hot and Sour Soup

Here it is: the favorite of Sichuan and Hunan aficionados everywhere. The seasoning is the key to the success of this gourmet's delight. Try it and you'll be amazed that something so good is so simple to make.

Before you start

Mix seasoning ingredients together in cup or small bowl. Mix marinade ingredients together in cup or small bowl. Soak dried crunchy mushrooms in 1 cup boiling water for 3 minutes.

1. Add ground meat to marinade in bowl and mix well. Set aside.

2. Pour chicken stock into saucepot, add marinated meat, and bring to boil.

3. As the soup stock is boiling, squeeze dry the crunchy mushrooms. By this time, they should be soft and have expanded to 5 times their original size. Remove hard particles and shred finely with Chinese cleaver or sharp knife. Set aside.

4. When stock boils, add tofu and mushrooms. Cook on high heat until soup comes to second boil.

5. Add seasoning and stir well. Add scallions and turn off heat.

6. Pour egg slowly into hot stock in thin stream. Stir again and mix well. Cover until ready to serve in individual soup bowls.

Seasoning

1 tablespoon cornstarch
1 teaspoon minced fresh garlic, or (TS)
   2 large cloves garlic, finely minced
½ teaspoon sugar
½ teaspoon black pepper
¼ teaspoon salt
2 tablespoons Worcestershire sauce
2 tablespoons cold water
2 tablespoons wine vinegar
1 tablespoon soy sauce
1 teaspoon sesame seed oil

Marinade

½ teaspoon cornstarch
¼ teaspoon sugar
1 tablespoon cold water
1 teaspoon soy sauce
½ teaspoon sesame seed oil
1 teaspoon dry sherry, gin, or
   vodka, optional

Ingredients

¼ cup presoaked crunchy (TS)
   mushrooms (won yee or cloud
   ears) or 1 tablespoon dried
   crunchy mushrooms
1 cup boiling water
¼ cup lean ground pork or beef
4 cups homemade chicken stock, (S)
   (p. 22), or 4 cups canned broth
½ cup firm tofu, drained and diced
2 tablespoons diced scallions, or (TS)
   1 scallion with green top, diced
1 egg, well beaten

measuring spoons and cups
large spoon
4 cups or small bowls
2-quart saucepot with lid
Chinese cleaver or sharp knife
cutting board
tray for ingredients
soup ladle
4 soup bowls

Note

This soup is easy to make ahead of time and reheat at dinnertime. For a hotter, spicier flavor, keep a bottle of hot chili sauce and a black pepper shaker on hand for diners to add to the soup.

Variation

For a vegetarian soup, use freshly made vegetable soup stock (p. 23) and omit the meat and marinade.

Yield: 4 to 6 servings

◆ *Entrees—Meats, Poultry, Seafood, Eggs, and Tofu* ◆

Chinese Meat Patties

A different but tasty way to make hamburgers—the Chinese way. The hamburgers, after marinating, can be broiled in a conventional oven, microwaved, or grilled. Beware: once your family tastes them, they will ask for more.

Before you start

Preheat oven to broil. Mix marinade ingredients together in large bowl.

1. Add ground beef and onion to marinade in bowl. With your hands or a wooden spoon, blend the marinade with the ingredients thoroughly. Separate meat into four equal portions. Shape each into a ball, then flatten into a patty.

2. Place beef patties on ungreased baking pan lined with double layers of aluminum foil to make cleanup easier.

3. For medium rare patties, broil in top rack of oven for 2 minutes on each side. Turn patties over once. For well done patties, double the broiling time.

Serve on hamburger buns or with rice or noodles, together with a salad or vegetable.

To microwave

Place the patties on a microwave-safe platter or in a shallow casserole dish and cover with paper towels. Microwave on high for 6 minutes for medium rare patties or 10 minutes for well done patties. Turn patties over once during cooking.

To grill

Grill for about 2 to 5 minutes on each side, depending on how well done you like your meat.

Note

This recipe can easily be doubled.

Yield: 4 servings

Marinade

1 tablespoon cornstarch
1/2 teaspoon sugar
1/4 teaspoon baking soda
1/4 teaspoon black pepper
2 tablespoons cold water
1 tablespoon soy sauce
1/2 tablespoon oyster sauce
1 tablespoon dry sherry, gin, or vodka, optional

Ingredients

1 pound lean ground chuck
1/2 tablespoon dried onion flakes or 1 medium onion, finely diced

Equipment

measuring spoons
wooden spoon
large bowl
9 x 13-inch or 8 x 8-inch baking pan
Chinese cleaver or sharp knife
cutting board
heavy-duty aluminum foil
tray for ingredients

Tender Beef Balls

Marinade

1 tablespoon cornstarch
½ teaspoon sugar
⅛ teaspoon baking soda
⅛ teaspoon white pepper
1 tablespoon cold water
1 teaspoon soy sauce
1 teaspoon oyster sauce
½ tablespoon sesame seed oil
½ tablespoon dry sherry, gin, or
   vodka, optional

Ingredients

boiling water for steamer
½ pound lean ground chuck,
   sirloin, or beef stew
½ tablespoon dried onion flakes
spinach leaves, enough to cover
   platter single-layered

Equipment

measuring spoons
wooden spoon
large bowl
13-inch Chinese steamer (or
   improvised steamer using a
   steamer rack and 14-inch wok
   or 4-quart saucepot with lid)
8-inch heat-proof plate with sides

Here is a new way of cooking ground beef—steamed! It is different, delectable, and easy. What's more, it is also low-fat and nutritious.

Before you start

Fill lower part of steamer to halfway mark with boiling water. Cover and bring to boil. Mix marinade in large bowl until smooth.

1. Add beef and onion flakes to marinade in bowl. Blend well with wooden spoon.

2. With wet hands, scoop 1 teaspoon of meat mixture and shape into a meatball. Continue to make meatballs until all meat is used.

3. Line a heat-proof plate with spinach. Place meatballs on leaves.

4. Place plate of meatballs on steamer rack. Place rack on steamer, cover, and steam on high for 7 to 8 minutes. Do not allow water in steamer to evaporate. Add boiling water as needed.

5. If using an improvised steamer, set plate of meatballs on steamer rack or inverted shallow bowl in the bottom of a large 4-quart saucepot or wok with lid. Add boiling water to fill bowl halfway. Cover pot with tight-fitting lid and steam over high heat for at least 10 minutes. Add boiling water as needed. If you use an improvised steamer, it will take longer to prepare this dish: the low water level in the pot will add to the cooking time.

Serve hot with a salad or vegetable, and hot rice or noodles.

Variation

Substitute lean ground pork for ground chuck and increase steaming time by 3 minutes to ensure that pork is properly cooked.

Yield: 2 to 4 servings (25 to 28 beef balls)

Beef and Peas

You have to taste it to believe just how delicious it is to pair ground beef with peas. A simple but tasty dish.

Before you start

Mix binder ingredients together in cup or small bowl. Mix marinade ingredients together in medium bowl.

1. Add beef to marinade in bowl and blend well. Set aside.

2. Soak peas in large bowl with boiling water to cover. Let stand 3 minutes to cook the peas. Drain.

3. Heat skillet or wok on high for 30 seconds. Add oil to coat skillet 30 seconds longer. Add minced garlic. Stir-toss for 15 seconds.

4. Add marinated beef and stir-toss for 2 minutes, until meat loses its pink color.

5. Add binder to beef and mix well. Fold in peas and mushrooms. Stir-toss for 1 minute longer.

Serve over hot rice or noodles, together with a salad or vegetable.

Yield: 4 to 6 servings

Binder

2 teaspoons cornstarch
¼ cup cold water

Marinade

1 teaspoon sugar
¼ teaspoon black pepper
¼ teaspoon baking powder
1 tablespoon soy sauce
1 tablespoon oyster sauce
1 tablespoon ketchup
1 tablespoon dry sherry, gin, or
    vodka, optional

Ingredients

1 pound lean ground chuck,
    sirloin, or beef stew
1 package (10-ounces) frozen
    green peas, well-thawed
3 cups boiling water
2 tablespoons corn, vegetable, or
    safflower oil, divided
½ teaspoon minced fresh garlic or (TS)
    1 large clove garlic, finely minced
1 can (4-ounces) small button
    mushrooms, drained

Equipment

measuring spoons and cups
slotted spoon, cup or small bowl
medium bowl, large bowl
10-inch skillet or 14-inch wok
Chinese cleaver or sharp knife
cutting board, serving platter
colander or strainer

Ants on the Hill

◆

A Chinese classic as intriguing as its name—ground beef glazed with oyster sauce resembles little ants, piled on a hill of cellophane noodles. You won't regret trying it.

Binder

2 teaspoons cornstarch

(S) ¼ cup chicken soup stock, freshly made (p. 22), or 4 cups canned chicken broth

Marinade

1 teaspoon sugar
¼ teaspoon black pepper
¼ teaspoon baking soda
2 tablespoons soy sauce
1 tablespoon oyster sauce
1 teaspoon sesame seed oil
1 tablespoon dry sherry, gin, or vodka, optional

Ingredients

1 pound lean ground chuck, sirloin, or beef stew

(TS) 3 cups fried cellophane noodles (p. 17)

3 tablespoons corn, vegetable, or safflower oil

(TS) 1 teaspoon minced fresh garlic or 2 large cloves garlic, minced

(TS) 2 tablespoons fresh scallions or 1 scallion with green top, diced

Equipment

measuring spoons and cups
large spoon or spatula
cup or small bowl, medium bowl
10-inch skillet or 14-inch wok
Chinese cleaver or sharp knife
cutting board, serving platter

Before you start

Mix binder ingredients in cup or small bowl until smooth. Set aside. Mix marinade ingredients together in medium bowl until smooth.

1. Add beef to marinade ingredients in bowl and blend well. Set aside.

2. Spread fried cellophane noodles evenly on serving platter.

3. Heat skillet or wok on high for 30 seconds. Add oil and swirl to coat skillet for 30 seconds longer. Add garlic. Stir-toss for 15 seconds. Add beef and marinade. Stir-toss for 2 minutes, until beef loses its pink color.

4. Add binder to beef in skillet and blend well. Cook for 1 minute.

5. Spoon cooked beef evenly over noodles. Garnish with scallions sprinkled on top.

Serve hot with rice and a salad or vegetable of your choice.

Yield: 4 to 6 servings

Hong Kong Steak

◆

Tired of steak the same old way? Try this—the Hong Kong way. It is robust and appealing.

Before you start
Mix sauce ingredients in cup or small bowl until smooth.

1. Line baking sheet with double layers of aluminum foil to make cleanup easier. Place steaks on baking sheet and sprinkle both sides with pepper. Set aside.

2. Peel and cut onions into half. Cut each half into quarters. Set aside. Wash and quarter mushrooms. Set aside.

3. Heat skillet or wok on high for 30 seconds. Add oil and swirl to coat skillet for 30 seconds longer. Add onions. Stir-toss for 1 to 2 minutes until they are translucent. Add mushrooms and stir-toss for 1 minute longer. Add sauce, blend well and bring to boil on low heat. Remove from heat, cover, and let stand.

4. Broil steaks, uncovered, on top oven rack 2 minutes each side for medium rare. For well done steaks, broil each side 4 to 5 minutes.

5. Transfer steaks to serving platter. Spoon sauce with onions and mushrooms over steaks and serve.

   Serve with rice or noodles and a salad or vegetable.

To grill
Grill steaks over high heat for 2 to 4 minutes on each side for rare steaks. For well done steaks, grill 4 to 6 minutes on each side.

Yield: 4 servings

Sauce
2 teaspoons cornstarch
1/2 teaspoon sugar
1/4 teaspoon black pepper
1 cup chicken soup stock, freshly (S) made (p. 22), or 1 cup canned chicken broth
2 tablespoons oyster sauce
2 tablespoons Worcestershire sauce
1 tablespoon dry sherry, gin, or vodka, optional

Ingredients
4 strip or porterhouse steaks, about 6 ounces each*
1/8 teaspoon black pepper
2 medium onions
12 fresh medium mushrooms
3 tablespoons corn, vegetable, or safflower oil

Equipment
measuring spoons and cups
large spoon or spatula
cup or small bowl
11 x 17-inch baking sheet
10-inch skillet or 14-inch wok with lid
Chinese cleaver or sharp knife
cutting board
heavy-duty aluminum foil
serving platter

*For steaks weighing more than 6 ounces, cut each one in half.

Hunan Beef with Potato Sticks

Ingredients

- 2 cans (1-ounce each) potato sticks
- 1 pound flank, round, or sirloin steak
- 3 tablespoons corn, vegetable, or safflower oil, divided
- (TS) 1 teaspoon fresh garlic or 2 large cloves garlic, finely minced
- 1 to 2 tablespoons Hunan chili paste or any brand of Chinese chili paste*
- (TS) 4 tablespoons diced fresh scallions or 2 scallions with green tops, diced

Binder

- (S) 3 tablespoons chicken soup stock, freshly made (p. 22) or 3 tablespoons canned chicken broth
- 2 tablespoons cold water
- 1 teaspoon cornstarch

Marinade

- 1 teaspoon sugar
- 1/4 teaspoon black pepper
- 1/4 teaspoon baking soda
- 2 tablespoons soy sauce
- 1 tablespoon oyster sauce
- 1 teaspoon sesame seed oil
- 1 tablespoon dry sherry, gin, or vodka, optional

A spicy delight! Here potato sticks are used as the "bed," on which is piled stir-fried beef spiked with hot sauce.

Before you start

Mix binder ingredients together in cup or small bowl. Mix marinade ingredients together in medium bowl. Spread potato sticks evenly on serving platter and set aside.

1. Slice beef across the grain into 2 x 1 x 1/8-inch thick slices. Add beef to marinade in bowl. Toss meat slices with marinade to coat well. Set aside.

2. Heat skillet or wok on high for 30 seconds. Add oil and swirl to coat skillet for 30 seconds longer. Add minced garlic and stir-toss for 15 seconds. Add Hunan chili paste, then beef and marinade. Stir-toss on high heat for 2 minutes until meat loses its pink color.

3. Add binder and scallions to skillet. Stir-toss for 1 minute. Spread beef evenly over potato sticks to serve.

This dish goes well with hot rice or noodles accompanied by a salad or vegetable.

Variation

Instead of potato sticks, use 2 cups of Fried Cellophane Noodles (p. 17) to line the platter.

Yield: 4 to 6 servings

Equipment

measuring spoons
large spoon or spatula
cup or small bowl
medium bowl
10-inch skillet or 14-inch wok
Chinese cleaver or sharp knife
cutting board
tray for ingredients
serving platter

The amount of chili paste you use depends on how hot you like it: fiery hot (2 to 3 tablespoons), medium hot (1 to 1½ tablespoons), or mild (½ tablespoon). Different brands vary in intensity of hotness. Experiment for best results.

Pepper Steak

◆

Binder

2 teaspoons cornstarch

(S) ¾ cup chicken soup stock, freshly
made (p. 22) or ¾ cup canned
chicken broth

2 tablespoons oyster sauce or
Worcestershire sauce

Marinade

1 teaspoon sugar
¼ teaspoon black pepper
¼ teaspoon baking soda
2 tablespoons soy sauce
1 teaspoon sesame seed oil
1 tablespoon dry sherry, gin, or
vodka, optional

Ingredients

2 (8-ounces each) strip or sirloin
steaks, well trimmed of fat and
bones
1 large green pepper
1 large onion
4 tablespoons corn, vegetable, or
safflower oil, divided
¼ teaspoon salt

Equipment

measuring spoons and cups
large spoon or spatula
cup or small bowl, large bowl
10-inch skillet or 14-inch wok
Chinese cleaver or sharp knife
cutting board
serving platter

Try this traditional favorite of meat lovers: a hearty blending of beef with green peppers. This is featured in many Chinese restaurants—now you can cook it yourself.

Before you start

Mix binder ingredients together in cup or small bowl. Mix marinade ingredients together in large bowl.

1. Cut steaks into 1-inch wide strips, then into 1-inch cubes (p. 20). Add steak cubes to marinade in large bowl and blend well. Set aside.

2. Wash and cut pepper in half, lengthwise. Scoop out seeds and cut off caps. Cut into 1-inch strips, then into 1-inch pieces. Set aside. Cut off both ends of onion and peel. Cut onion in half, then each half into quarters. Set aside.

3. Heat skillet or wok on high for 30 seconds. Add 2 tablespoons oil and swirl to coat skillet for 30 seconds longer. Add onions and pepper. Stir-toss for 1 minute. Add salt and blend well. Remove to serving platter.

4. Swirl 2 tablespoons oil in hot skillet for 30 seconds. Add beef cubes and marinade. Stir-toss for 3 to 4 minutes or until meat loses its pink color. Add onions and peppers to beef and mix well.

5. Add well-mixed binder to skillet and blend well. Stir-toss for 1 minute longer. Transfer to serving platter.

Serve over hot rice or noodles, together with a salad or vegetable.

Yield: 4 servings

Roast Pork with Peapods and Bamboo Shoots

A tasty dish for any season and convenient when you have a batch of cooked roast pork ready. Crunchy peapods complement the flavor of the pork.

Before you start

Mix binder ingredients together in cup or small bowl.

1. Thin-slice roast pork strips diagonally (p. 24) and set aside.

2. If using fresh peapods, snip off top end with kitchen shears. Wash, drain, and set aside.

3. Heat skillet or wok on high for 30 seconds. Add 1½ tablespoons oil and swirl to coat skillet for 30 seconds longer. Add peapods and stir-toss for 1 minute. Add bamboo shoots and salt. Blend well and cook for 1 minute longer. Remove contents to platter.

4. Swirl remaining oil (1½ tablespoons) in hot skillet for 30 seconds. Add scallions and roast pork slices. Stir-toss for 1 minute. Add binder. Blend for 1 minute longer on high until gravy bubbles. Add peapods and bamboo shoots. Mix and remove to serving platter.

This dish goes well with rice or noodles, accompanied by a salad or vegetable.

Yield: 4 servings

Binder

1 teaspoon cornstarch
⅓ cup chicken soup stock, freshly (S) made (p. 22) or ⅓ cup canned chicken broth
½ tablespoon oyster sauce

Ingredients

1 strip roast pork (p. 24), about (S) ¼ pound
½ pound fresh edible peapods or 1 package (6-ounces) frozen peapods, thawed
3 tablespoons corn, vegetable, or safflower oil, divided
⅔ cup sliced bamboo shoots
¼ teaspoon salt
2 tablespoons diced fresh scallions (TS) or 1 scallion with green top, diced

Equipment

measuring spoons and cups
large spoon or spatula
cup or small bowl
10-inch skillet or 14-inch wok
Chinese cleaver or sharp knife
cutting board
kitchen shears
colander or strainer
tray for ingredients
serving platter

Roast Pork with Tofu

◆

Binder

1 teaspoon cornstarch
¼ teaspoon salt
¼ cup cold water
(S) ¼ cup chicken soup stock, freshly
   made (p. 22) or ¼ cup canned
   chicken broth
1 tablespoon oyster sauce

Ingredients

(S) 1 strip roast pork (p. 24), about
   ¼ pound
1 pound firm tofu, drained
3 tablespoons corn, vegetable, or
   safflower oil, divided
(TS) ½ teaspoon minced fresh garlic or
   1 large clove garlic, finely
   minced
(TS) 2 tablespoons diced fresh scallions
   or 1 scallion with green top,
   diced
½ can (16-ounces) straw
   mushrooms drained

Equipment

measuring spoons and cups
large spoon or spatula
medium bowl
10-inch skillet or 14-inch wok
Chinese cleaver or sharp knife
cutting board
colander or strainer
serving platter

Guaranteed to please with no leftovers if you marry tasty roast pork with tofu. Try this for yourself and prove it.

Before you start

Mix binder ingredients together in medium bowl until smooth.

1. Thin-slice roast pork strip diagonally (p. 24) and set aside.

2. Slice tofu into 1 x 1 x ½-inch slices. Drain in colander again to remove excess water. Set aside.

3. Heat skillet or wok on high for 30 seconds. Add 1½ tablespoons oil and swirl to coat skillet for 30 seconds longer. Add garlic and roast pork slices. Stir-toss for 1 minute. Remove to platter.

4. Swirl remaining oil in hot skillet for 30 seconds. Add diced scallions and tofu slices. Stir-toss for 1 minute. Add straw mushrooms and roast pork to skillet. Blend well for 1 minute. Add binder. Blend for 1 minute longer on high until gravy bubbles. Remove to serving platter.

This dish goes well with rice or noodles, accompanied by a salad or vegetable.

Yield: 4 servings

Chicken, Agar-Agar, and Peapods

A unique taste combination—agar-agar strips. Surprise your family and friends and they will in turn surprise you with their applause.

Before you start
Combine dressing ingredients in small jar with lid and shake well. Chill salad plates in freezer until ready to use.

1. Cut agar-agar strips into 2-inch lengths and soak in 2 cups hot water in a medium bowl for 2 minutes. Drain well and set aside.

2. Wash fresh peapods and snip off top ends with kitchen shears. Soak in 2 cups boiling water for 1 minute. Drain and refresh in cold water to stop cooking. Set aside. If using frozen peapods, just rinse in hot water, drain, and set aside.

3. Combine shredded chicken, agar-agar strips, and peapods in large salad bowl. Pour dressing over chicken mixture and toss to coat.

Serve on chilled salad plates, together with fried rice (p. 101–04), noodles (p. 17), or in sandwiches.

Note
To make this salad, use only agar-agar strips, not agar-agar flakes or squares.

Yield: 4 servings

Dressing
½ teaspoon sugar
½ teaspoon Dijon mustard
¼ teaspoon white pepper
¼ cup sesame seed oil
2 tablespoons soy sauce

Ingredients
1 cup dried agar-agar strips
2 cups hot water
6 ounces (about 45) edible
    peapods, or 1 package
    (6-ounces) frozen peapods,
    well-thawed
2 cups boiling water
1 cup No-work Chicken (p. 26), (S)
    shredded

Equipment
measuring spoons and cups
large spoon
medium bowl
large salad bowl
kitchen shears
colander or strainer
small jar with lid
salad plates

Dragon and Phoenix in the Forest

Binder

2 teaspoons cornstarch
¼ teaspoon salt
¼ teaspoon white pepper
3 tablespoons cold water

Ingredients

1 bunch fresh broccoli spears,
   washed
4 cups boiling water
(S) ½ No-work Chicken (p. 26)
8 ounces boiled ham, sliced
   ⅛-inch thick
(S) 1 cup chicken soup stock, freshly
   made (p. 22), or 1 cup canned
   chicken broth

Equipment

measuring spoons and cups
large spoon
cup or small bowl
2-quart saucepot
4-quart saucepot
Chinese cleaver or sharp knife
cutting board
colander or strainer
serving platter

A beautiful dish to prepare and eat. The green broccoli florets contrast beautifully with the chicken and ham. What's more, truly a banquet dish: traditionally served to very special guests on very special occasions.

Before you start

Mix binder ingredients together in cup or small bowl until smooth.

1. Cut broccoli florets into pieces 2½-inches long. Discard the stalks. Parboil florets in 4 cups boiling water for 3 minutes until they are crunchy to the bite. Drain and immediately soak in cold water for 5 minutes to stop cooking. Drain well and set aside.

2. Cut 2 x 1 x ⅛-inch slices from No-work Chicken. Stack slices neatly in a pile. Save chicken carcass to use in making soup later.

3. Cut ham slices into the same size strips and stack neatly in a separate pile.

4. Arrange broccoli florets in a row around the edge of a serving platter with florets facing outwards. Alternate ham and chicken slices in the middle of platter in a symmetrical pattern until all slices are used or platter is filled.

5. In small saucepot bring chicken stock to boil. Add binder to boiling broth and stir until smooth and thickened.

6. Slowly pour sauce over chicken, ham, and broccoli.

Serve hot, together with hot rice or noodles and a salad of your choice.

Yield: 4 to 6 servings

Turkey with Zucchinis

◆

A delicate dish—combining turkey with zucchini, spiked with a gentle taste of oyster sauce. See how well the two ingredients blend when you try this dish.

Before you start

Mix binder ingredients together in cup or small bowl. Mix marinade ingredients together in medium bowl.

1. Slice turkey cutlets or boneless breasts into thin slices (p. 19). Add to marinade in bowl and mix well. Set aside.

2. Wash zucchinis and cut off both ends. Cut into ¼-inch rounds. Set aside.

3. Heat skillet or wok on high for 30 seconds. Add 1 tablespoon oil and swirl to coat skillet for 30 seconds longer. Add zucchinis and salt. Stir-toss for 30 seconds. Add water, cover, and cook for 1 minute longer. Remove zucchinis to platter and set aside.

4. Swirl 3 tablespoons oil in hot skillet for 30 seconds. Add minced garlic and stir-toss for 15 seconds. Add turkey slices and marinade. Stir-toss for 2 minutes until meat loses its pink color. Add scallions and binder. Stir-toss for 1 minute longer.

5. Add reserved zucchinis and stir-toss with turkey for 1 minute. Mix well.

Transfer to serving platter and serve immediately over hot rice or noodles, together with a salad or vegetable.

Variation

Boneless, skinless chicken breasts may be substituted for the turkey.

Yield: 4 to 6 servings

Binder

1 teaspoon cornstarch
2 tablespoons cold water
1 tablespoon oyster sauce

Marinade

½ teaspoon sugar
½ teaspoon baking soda
¼ teaspoon salt
¼ teaspoon white pepper
1 tablespoon sesame seed oil
1 tablespoon dry sherry, gin, or vodka, optional

Ingredients

½ pound raw turkey cutlets or boneless, skinless turkey breasts
2 medium zucchinis
4 tablespoons corn, vegetable, or safflower oil, divided
½ teaspoon salt
¼ cup cold water
1 teaspoon garlic or 2 large (TS) cloves garlic, finely minced
2 tablespoons diced fresh scallions (TS) or 1 scallion with green top, diced

Equipment

measuring spoons and cups
large spoon or spatula
cup or small bowl, medium bowl
10-inch skillet or 14-inch wok
Chinese cleaver or sharp knife
cutting board, serving platter
tray for ingredients

Diced Chicken with Peas and Mushrooms

Binder

1 teaspoon cornstarch
2 tablespoons cold water

Marinade

½ teaspoon sugar
½ teaspoon salt
½ teaspoon baking soda
¼ teaspoon white pepper
1 tablespoon sesame seed oil
1 tablespoon dry sherry, gin, or
    vodka, optional

Ingredients

½ pound fresh chicken nuggets or
    2 boneless chicken breasts
    (about ½ pound), with skin and
    fat removed
4 tablespoons corn, vegetable, or
    safflower oil, divided
1 small onion, cut into ½-inch
    pieces
1 package (10-ounces) frozen
    peas, well-thawed
1 can (4-ounces) button
    mushrooms, drained
½ teaspoon salt
(TS) 1 teaspoon minced fresh garlic or
    2 large cloves garlic, minced
1 to 2 tablespoons Hunan chili
    paste, or any brand of Chinese
    chili paste, optional*

Try this dish mild or spicy. For the mild version, do not add Hunan chili paste. For the spicy version, add 1 to 2 tablespoons Hunan chili paste. Either version is delicious and your guests will ask for more.

Before you start

Mix binder ingredients together in cup or small bowl. Mix marinade ingredients together in medium bowl.

1. Cut chicken nuggets or chicken breasts into ½-inch cubes (p. 20). Add chicken cubes to marinade in medium bowl. Blend well and set aside.

2. Heat skillet or wok on high for 30 seconds. Add 2 tablespoons oil and swirl to coat skillet for 30 seconds longer. Add onion. Stir-toss for 1 minute. Add peas, mushrooms, and salt. Stir-toss for 2 minutes longer. Remove vegetables to platter and set aside.

3. Swirl 2 tablespoons oil in hot skillet for 30 seconds. Add minced garlic and Hunan hot sauce, if desired. Stir-toss for 30 seconds. Add chicken cubes and marinade. Stir-toss for 2 minutes until meat loses its pink color.

4. Add reserved vegetables and stir-toss with chicken for 1 to 2 minutes longer. Add binder and mix well.

Serve immediately over hot rice or noodles, together with a salad or vegetable.

Note

½ cup sliced fresh mushrooms may be substituted for the canned variety. Washing and slicing the mushrooms will add several more minutes to the preparation time.

Variation

1 cup fresh peapods may be substituted for the peas.

Yield: 4 to 6 servings

Equipment

measuring spoons
large spoon or spatula
cup or small bowl
medium bowl
10-inch skillet or 14-inch wok
Chinese cleaver or sharp knife
cutting board
colander or strainer
serving platter

*The amount of chili paste you use depends on how hot you like it: fiery hot (2 to 3 tablespoons), medium hot (1 to 1½ tablespoons), or mild (½ tablespoon). Different brands vary in intensity of hotness. Experiment for best results.

Spicy Chicken with Cashews

◆

Marinade

1½ teaspoons sugar

1 teaspoon cornstarch

¼ teaspoon baking soda

2 tablespoons soy sauce

1½ tablespoons sesame seed oil

1 tablespoon Worcestershire sauce

1 tablespoon water

2 tablespoons dry sherry, gin, or
    vodka, optional

Yu Hsiang Seasoning

1 to 2 tablespoons Hunan chili
    paste or any brand of Chinese
    chili paste*

(TS) 2 tablespoons diced fresh scallions
    or 1 scallion with green top,
    diced

(TS) 1 teaspoon minced fresh garlic or
    2 large cloves garlic, finely
    minced

(TS) 1 teaspoon grated fresh gingerroot

Ingredients

½ pound fresh chicken nuggets or
    2 boneless chicken breasts
    (about ½ pound), with skin and
    fat removed

1 large green or red pepper

3 tablespoons corn, vegetable, or
    safflower oil

1 cup dry roasted whole cashews

This spicy hot dish will be welcomed by diners who like spicy food. The hot sauce with gingerroot, scallions, and garlic is adapted from the traditional "Yu Hsiang" method of cooking, famous in Sichuan. "Yu Hsiang," translated literally, means "fish fragrant." This dish, however, is by no means fishy. On the contrary, it is fragrantly spicy and a good "rice-sender," that is, diners gobble down many bowls of rice.

Before you start

Mix marinade ingredients together in medium bowl. Mix Yu Hsiang seasoning ingredients together in cup or small bowl.

1. Cut chicken into ½-inch cubes (see p. 20). Add to marinade ingredients in bowl and toss to coat well. Set aside. Marinating longer will enhance the flavor of the chicken.

2. Wash and cut pepper in half, lengthwise. Scoop out seeds and cut off caps. Cut into ½-inch slices, then into ½-inch pieces (p. 20). Set aside.

3. Heat skillet or wok on high for 30 seconds. Swirl oil in hot skillet for 30 seconds. Add Yu Hsiang seasoning. Stir-toss for 15 seconds. Add chicken and marinade. Stir-toss for 2 to 3 minutes until chicken loses its pink color.

4. Add cashews and green pepper. Blend and cook for 1 minute. Transfer to serving platter.

This dish goes well with rice or noodles, together with a light soup and vegetable.

Variation
Substitute raw shelled peanuts for the cashews.

Yield: 4 servings

Equipment

measuring spoons and cups
large spoon or spatula
cup or small bowl
medium bowl
10-inch skillet or 14-inch wok
  with lid
Chinese cleaver or sharp knife
cutting board
grater

*The amount of chili paste you use depends on how hot you like it: fiery hot (2 to 3 tablespoons), medium hot (1 to 1½ tablespoons), or mild (½ tablespoon). Different brands vary in intensity of hotness. Experiment for best results.

Steamed Boston Scrod Fillet

◆

Seasoning

¼ teaspoon salt
¼ teaspoon sugar
¼ teaspoon white pepper
1 tablespoon corn, vegetable, or
* safflower oil*
1 tablespoon soy sauce
1 tablespoon dry sherry, gin, or
* vodka, optional*

Ingredients

boiling water for steamer
1 pound boneless Boston scrod
* fillet, cut into 4 portions*
(TS) *4 medium fresh mushrooms,*
* washed and finely sliced or 4*
* presoaked Chinese dried black*
* mushrooms (p. 16)*
(TS) *2 tablespoons fresh scallions or 1*
* scallion with green top, diced*
(TS) *½ tablespoon grated fresh*
* gingerroot*

Equipment

measuring spoons, large spoon
cup or small bowl
13-inch Chinese steamer (or
* improvised steamer using a*
* steamer rack and 14-inch wok*
* or 4-quart saucepot with lid)*
Chinese cleaver or sharp knife
cutting board, grater
heat-proof platter with deep sides
paper towels

Boston scrod cooked in this way can be just as tender, flaky, and sweet as that served in the best restaurants.

Before you start

Mix seasoning ingredients. Fill lower part of steamer to halfway with boiling water. Cover and bring water to a rolling boil.

1. Wash and pat dry fish. Place on heat-proof platter. Spread mushrooms, scallions, and gingerroot over top of fillet. Pour seasoning over fish.

2. Place plate of fish on steamer rack. Place rack on steamer, cover, and steam on high for 8 minutes. Do not allow water in steamer to evaporate. Replenish with boiling water as needed to maintain a constant water level.

3. If using an improvised steamer, set the plate of fish on a steamer rack or inverted shallow bowl in the bottom of a large 4-quart saucepot or wok with lid. Add boiling water to about halfway up sides of bowl. Cover the pot with a tight-fitting lid and steam fish over high heat for about 10 minutes. Do not allow water to evaporate. Replenish with boiling water as needed to maintain a constant water level. If you use an improvised steamer, it will take longer to prepare this dish because the low water level in the pot will add to the cooking time.

Serve fish immediately in sauce on plate. This dish goes well with hot rice, accompanied by a vegetable of your choice.

Variation

Fillet of sole can be substituted for the Boston scrod.

Yield: 4 servings

Shrimp Steamed in the Shell

Succulent shrimp steamed in the classic tradition of Shanghai. The sweet taste of fresh shrimp is recaptured in this simple recipe.

Before you start

Fill lower part of steamer halfway with boiling water. Cover and bring to boil. Mix dipping sauce ingredients in bowl and set aside.

1. Wash shrimp, drain, but do not peel shell. With kitchen shears, make a shallow cut along back shell of each shrimp to make it easier for diners to peel shrimp. Place shrimp in heat-proof platter. Add cornstarch to shrimp and mix well with hands.

2. Place plate of shrimp on steamer rack. Place rack on steamer, cover, and steam on high for 5 minutes, until shrimp turns pink. Do not allow water in steamer to evaporate. Replenish with boiling water as needed to maintain a constant water level.

3. If using an improvised steamer, set the plate of shrimp on a steamer rack or inverted shallow bowl in the bottom of a large 4-quart saucepot or wok with lid. Add boiling water to about halfway up sides of bowl. Cover the pot with a tight-fitting lid and steam shrimp over high heat for 7 to 8 minutes. Do not allow water to evaporate. Replenish with boiling water as needed to maintain a constant water level. If you use an improvised steamer, it will take longer to prepare this dish because the low water level in the pot will add to the cooking time.

Serve immediately with sauce. Diners peel the shrimp and spoon dipping sauce over shrimp on their plates.

Note

Leftover sauce can be refrigerated in a covered jar for several weeks.

Yield: 4 servings

Dipping Sauce

¼ *cup soy sauce*
¼ *cup wine vinegar*
1 *tablespoon sesame seed oil*
2 *tablespoons diced fresh scallions* (TS)
   or 1 scallion with green top, diced
½ *tablespoon grated fresh* (TS)
   gingerroot
½ *teaspoon minced fresh garlic or* (TS)
   1 large clove garlic, finely minced

Ingredients

boiling water for steamer
20 *to* 25 *large shrimp in shell (about 1 pound), raw*
1 *teaspoon cornstarch*

Equipment

measuring spoons and cups
large spoon
sauce bowl or gravy boat
13-*inch Chinese steamer (or improvised steamer using a steamer-rack and 14-inch wok or 4-quart saucepot with lid)*
Chinese cleaver or sharp knife
cutting board
grater
kitchen shears
colander or strainer
heat-proof platter with deep sides

Five-spice Salmon with Garlic

Marinade

½ teaspoon five-spice powder
2 tablespoons soy sauce
1 tablespoon corn, vegetable, or
    safflower oil
(TS) 2 tablespoons diced fresh scallions
    or 1 scallion with green top,
    diced
(TS) 1 teaspoon minced fresh garlic, or
    2 large cloves garlic, finely
    minced
(TS) ½ teaspoon grated fresh
    gingerroot
2 tablespoons dry sherry, gin, or
    vodka, optional

Ingredient

4 fresh salmon, cod, or halibut
    steaks, about ½-inch thick and
    about 5 ounces each

Equipment

measuring spoons
large spoon
cup or small bowl
9 x 13-inch baking pan
Chinese cleaver or sharp knife
cutting board
pastry brush
heavy-duty aluminum foil

Five-spice powder, a combination of star anise, fennel, cloves, cinnamon, and peppercorn adds a special taste and dimension to the salmon.

Before you start

Preheat oven to broil. Mix marinade ingredients together in cup or small bowl.

1. Line baking pan with double layers of aluminum foil to make cleanup easier. Place salmon steaks side by side in pan. Pour marinade over salmon.

2. Broil salmon steaks, uncovered, on top rack in oven for 2 to 3 minutes. Turn steaks. Brush with marinade in pan and broil for another 2 to 3 minutes.

Serve salmon with gravy over rice or noodles, together with a salad or vegetable.

Yield: 4 servings

Baked Fillets of Sole

Scallions and ginger, combined with salt and hot oil, add an elegant twist to the sole. Different and delicious!

Before you start

Preheat oven to 350° for 5 minutes. Mix marinade ingredients in cup or small bowl.

1. Place sole fillets on baking sheet lined with double layers of aluminum foil to make cleanup easier. Spread marinade on both sides of sole fillets with pastry brush and set aside. Let stand for 2 minutes.

2. Place scallions, gingerroot, and salt in medium bowl and set aside.

3. Bake sole, uncovered, for 4 to 5 minutes. Turn fillets and bake for another 4 to 5 minutes on other side.

4. While the fillets are in the oven, heat ¼ cup oil in saucepot until almost smoking, about 375°, for about 3 minutes. Pour hot oil over scallion-ginger mixture.

5. Transfer fillets to serving platter. Spoon scallion-ginger sauce over sole.

   Serve, together with rice or noodles, accompanied by a salad or vegetable.

Variation

Substitute whitefish, pickerel, or other boneless fresh fillets for the sole.

Yield: 4 servings

Marinade

½ teaspoon salt
¼ teaspoon white pepper
1 tablespoon dry sherry, gin, or
   vodka, optional

Ingredients

1 pound (4 pieces) boneless sole
   fillets
4 tablespoons diced fresh scallions (TS)
   or 2 scallions with green tops,
   diced
2 teaspoons grated fresh (TS)
   gingerroot
1 teaspoon salt
¼ cup corn, vegetable, or
   safflower oil

Equipment

measuring spoons and cups
large spoon
cup or small bowl
medium bowl
11 x 17-inch baking sheet
1½-quart saucepot
Chinese cleaver, or sharp knife
cutting board
pastry brush
grater
heavy-duty aluminum foil
serving platter

Fish Steamed in Microwave

―――――――――◆―――――――――

Ingredients

2 scallions with green tops
6 slices of fresh unpeeled
  gingerroot, each about
  size of a 50-cent piece
1 whole fresh pickerel, pike, or
  whitefish (about 1½ pounds),
  scaled and cleaned, but with
  head, eyes, tail, and fins intact
¼ cup corn, vegetable, or
  safflower oil
¼ cup soy sauce

Equipment

measuring spoons and cups
large spoon
1½-quart saucepot
Chinese cleaver or sharp knife
cutting board
timer
paper towels
plastic wrap
toothpick or thin bamboo skewer
oval heat-proof serving platter

This classic fish is traditionally served on birthdays and weddings. Fish is the homonym in Chinese for long life and abundance. Cooking the fish in the microwave is just like steaming because it retains the moisture. Fish cooked this way captures the essence of the sea. Prepare it for your family and friends and earn your crown as a master chef!

Before you start

Wash scallions, discard roots, fine-sliver, and set aside. Fine-sliver ginger and set aside.

1. Dry fish with paper towels. Place fish on its side on cutting board. With sharp knife, score skin by making diagonal cuts about 1-inch apart, ½-inch deep down its length from head to tail. This will ensure even cooking. Turn fish over and score other side in the same manner.

2. Place fish on its side on oval heat-proof serving platter. Cover with a large sheet of plastic wrap. Cook on high for 6 minutes. At the end of 6 minutes, check if done by inserting a toothpick or thin bamboo skewer into middle part of fish. If fish is done, the toothpick will come out clean and the flesh will feel tender to the touch.

3. Discard cooking juice. Spread slivered scallions and gingerroot evenly over fish.

4. In dry and clean saucepot, heat ¼ cup of oil until almost smoking, about 375°. Pour hot oil over scallions and gingerroot in a thin stream. Add soy sauce.

Serve immediately. The fish can easily be flaked off with a fork and knife or with chopsticks. Serve together with slivers of scallions and gingerroot with some gravy. This dish goes well with hot rice and a stir-fried vegetable.

Note

Only the freshest fish can be prepared in this way. Ask your grocer or fishmonger to dress the dish this way: keep eyes, fins, and tail intact. Just scale, remove the gills and innards but nothing else. Also ask that it be dressed without breaking the bile.

Yield: 4 servings

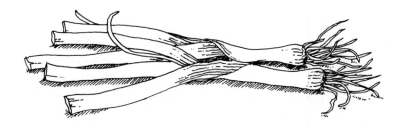

Shrimp in the Shell with Spicy Sauce

———————— ◆ ————————

Seasoning

1 teaspoon sugar
¼ teaspoon black pepper
(S) ½ cup chicken stock, (p. 22),
    or ½ cup canned broth
¼ cup ketchup
2 tablespoons Worcestershire sauce
1 tablespoon soy sauce
1 tablespoon oyster sauce

Binder

2 teaspoons cornstarch
2 tablespoons cold water

Ingredients

1 pound medium or large shrimp
    in the shell, raw
4 tablespoons corn, vegetable, or
    safflower oil
¼ teaspoon salt
(TS) 1 teaspoon grated fresh gingerroot
(TS) 1 teaspoon minced fresh garlic or
    2 large cloves garlic, minced
(TS) 4 tablespoons fresh scallions or 2
    scallions with green tops, diced

Equipment

measuring spoons and cups
large spoon or spatula
cup or small bowl, medium bowl
10-inch skillet or 14-inch wok
Chinese cleaver or sharp knife
cutting board, grater, colander,
    paper towels, serving platter

Shrimp in a spicy sauce! As an entree for a very special meal, you cannot top this.

Before you start

Mix seasoning ingredients together in medium bowl. Mix binder ingredients together in cup or small bowl.

1. Wash shrimp, drain, and dry with paper towels. Do not peel shell.

2. Heat skillet or wok on high for 30 seconds. Add oil and swirl to coat skillet for 30 seconds longer. Add salt, gingerroot, and garlic. Stir-toss for 15 seconds.

3. Add shrimp and stir-toss for 1 to 2 minutes until they turn pink but are not burned.

4. Add seasoning to shrimp. Blend well for 1 minute. Add scallions. Stir-toss for one minute longer. When sauce comes to a boil, add binder. Blend and stir-toss. Spoon to serving platter.

    Serve together with another entree, accompanied by hot rice or noodles, and a salad or vegetable.

Note

This dish can be cooked ahead of time and served cold.

Variation

This dish can also be prepared with 2 tablespoons of either dry sherry, gin, or vodka for extra richness.

Yield: 4 servings

Stir-fried Sichuan Shrimp

Shrimp spiked with Chinese hot sauce are delectable. Serve this exciting dish on a dull day.

Before you start

Mix binder ingredients together in cup or small bowl. Mix marinade ingredients together in medium bowl until smooth.

1. Add shrimp to marinade in bowl. Mix well and set aside.

2. Soak peas in large bowl with 3 cups boiling water to cover. After 3 minutes, drain, and set aside.

3. Heat skillet or wok on high for 30 seconds. Add oil to coat skillet for 30 seconds longer. Add Hunan chili paste. Stir-toss for 15 seconds. Add shrimp and marinade. Stir-toss for 2 minutes until they are just cooked. Add binder and blend well.

4. Add peas and scallions. Mix and stir-toss for 1 minute and serve.

   Serve with rice or noodles, soup, and another entree.

Note

The amount of chili paste you use depends on how hot you like it: fiery hot (2 to 3 tablespoons), medium hot (1 to 1½ tablespoons), mild (½ tablespoon). Different brands vary in intensity of hotness. Experiment for best results.

Variation

For a mild taste, substitute oyster sauce for Hunan chili paste. Add 1 tablespoon oyster sauce to binder; follow same directions. For richer taste, add ½ tablespoon dry sherry, gin, or vodka to marinade.

Yield: 4 servings

Binder

1 teaspoon cornstarch
2 tablespoons cold water

Marinade

½ teaspoon salt
½ teaspoon sugar
½ teaspoon baking soda
¼ teaspoon cornstarch
1 tablespoon corn, vegetable, or safflower oil
¼ teaspoon grated gingerroot (TS)

Ingredients

1 pound fresh or frozen shrimp, shelled, deveined, and well-thawed
1 package (10-ounces) frozen green peas, well-thawed
3 cups boiling water
4 tablespoons corn, vegetable, or safflower oil
1 tablespoon Hunan chili paste or any brand of Chinese chili paste
4 tablespoons fresh scallions or 2 (TS) scallions with green tops, diced

Equipment

measuring spoons and cups
large spoon or spatula
small, medium, and large bowls
10-inch skillet or 14-inch wok
Chinese cleaver or sharp knife
cutting board, grater
colander, serving platter

Stir-fried Scallops with Asparagus

Asparagus stir-fried with scallops is one of the most delicate dishes.

Before you start

Mix sauce ingredients in cup or small bowl until smooth.

Sauce

1 teaspoon cornstarch
¼ teaspoon sugar
¼ teaspoon baking soda
⅛ teaspoon white pepper
2 tablespoons cold water
½ tablespoon oyster sauce
½ tablespoon sesame seed oil
(TS) 2 tablespoons fresh scallions or 1
   scallion with green top, diced
½ tablespoon dry sherry, gin, or
   vodka, optional

1. Wash asparagus stalks and snap off tough ends. The stalks usually break at the woody part of the stem. Discard ends. Slice stalks diagonally (p. 20) into 2-inch lengths. Set aside.

2. Wash scallops, drain, and dry well with paper towels.

3. Heat skillet or wok on high for 30 seconds. Add 2 tablespoons oil to coat skillet for 30 seconds longer. Add garlic and salt. Stir-toss for 15 seconds. Add asparagus. Stir-toss for 1 minute. Add 2 tablespoons cold water and cook for 1 minute longer. Remove to serving platter.

Ingredients

1 pound fresh asparagus
½ pound fresh sea or bay
   scallops, uncooked
4 tablespoons corn, vegetable, or
   safflower oil, divided
(TS) 1 teaspoon minced fresh garlic or
   2 large cloves garlic, finely
   minced
½ teaspoon salt
2 tablespoons cold water
(TS) 1 teaspoon grated fresh gingerroot

4. Swirl 2 tablespoons oil in hot skillet for 30 seconds. Add gingerroot and stir-fry for 15 seconds. Add scallops. Stir-toss for about 2 minutes until they are cooked. Add sauce. Stir-toss for 30 seconds. Add reserved asparagus. Blend well. Transfer to serving platter.

This dish goes well with rice or noodles, accompanied by a soup and another entree of your choice.

Yield: 4 to 6 servings

Equipment

measuring spoons
large spoon or spatula
cup or small bowl
10-inch skillet or 14-inch wok
Chinese cleaver or sharp knife
cutting board, grater
colander or strainer
paper towels, serving platter

Egg Pouch

An egg dish fit for king or commoner alike. Both love it and claim it worthy of them. Your family will too!

Before you start

Mix seasoning ingredients in cup or small bowl.

1. Heat skillet or wok on high for 30 seconds. Add ½ tablespoon oil and swirl to coat skillet for 30 seconds longer. Carefully break 1 egg into hot oil. When white is set, in about 1 minute, gently fold half the egg over to meet the other half. Gently press the egg's edges together to seal the pouch. When yolk is set, about 1 minute, remove egg to plate. It takes patience to keep the yolk intact. If it breaks, let cook 1 minute longer, then fold. It will be just as tasty.

2. Follow the same procedure for the remaining 3 eggs. If the skillet gets too hot, turn heat to medium high.

3. Carefully return all 4 eggs one by one into hot skillet and place them side by side. Sprinkle scallions and pour seasoning on top. Cover skillet and turn heat to low. Cook for 3 minutes longer to combine flavors.

Serve over hot rice with a salad or vegetable dish and another entree.

Note

The classic egg pouch is formed at the "easy over" step. One half of the egg is folded to meet the other half, and the edges are gently pressed to seal the pouch. To keep the yolk intact, each step must be followed carefully and slowly.

Yield: 2 to 4 servings

Seasoning

¾ teaspoon sugar
⅛ teaspoon black pepper
2 tablespoons soy sauce
3 tablespoons cold water
1 tablespoon dry sherry, gin, or
   vodka, optional

Ingredients

2 tablespoons corn, vegetable, or
   safflower oil (or ½ tablespoon
   per egg)
4 large eggs, at room temperature
4 tablespoons diced fresh scallions (TS)
   or 2 scallions with green tops,
   diced

Equipment

measuring spoons
large spoon and spatula
cup or small bowl
10-inch skillet or 14-inch wok
   with lid
Chinese cleaver or sharp knife
cutting board
serving platter

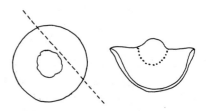

Bean Sprout Pancakes

———— ◆ ————

Unpretentious but good describes this recipe for bean sprouts and eggs. It is easy to make and is a real treat for the vegetarian and meat lover too.

Seasoning

½ teaspoon salt
½ teaspoon sugar
¼ teaspoon white pepper
1 teaspoon sesame seed oil

Ingredients

4 eggs, well beaten
1 cup fresh bean sprouts, washed and drained
(TS) 2 tablespoons diced fresh scallions or 1 scallion with green top, diced
(TS) ½ teaspoon minced fresh garlic or 1 large clove garlic, finely minced
2 tablespoons corn, vegetable, or safflower oil

Equipment

measuring spoons and cups
large spoon and spatula
cup or small bowl
large bowl
10-inch skillet or 14-inch wok
Chinese cleaver or sharp knife
cutting board
chopsticks or fork
serving platter

Before you start

Mix seasoning ingredients together in cup or small bowl.

1. Mix beaten eggs with bean sprouts, scallions, and garlic in large bowl. Add seasoning and blend well.

2. Heat skillet or wok on high for 30 seconds. Add ½ tablespoon oil and swirl to coat skillet for 15 seconds longer. Spoon ⅓ cup of egg-sprout mixture into skillet and tilt skillet so that egg mixture is spread evenly.

3. Fry pancake for 1 to 1½ minutes until golden brown and egg is set. Turn and fry on the other side for about 1 minute or so until pancake is set. Remove to platter. If skillet gets too hot, turn heat to medium high.

4. Repeat with remaining egg-sprout mixture until all is used, and you have 4 pancakes.

Serve hot with rice, or roll pancakes as crepes and serve with a salad. These pancakes can also be served as a filling for pita bread or sandwiches.

Note

This dish can double as a luncheon item by itself or as an entree at dinner.

Yield: 2 to 4 servings (4 pancakes)

Tofu with Three Spices

At last fresh gingerroot and its sisters, garlic and scallions, get the special treatment they deserve! Here combined with tofu, they impart that special taste to make this dish unforgettable.

Before you start

Mix seasoning ingredients together in cup or small bowl until smooth.

1. Cut tofu into 1 x 1 x ½-inch slices. Drain in colander again to remove excess water. Set aside.

2. Heat skillet or wok on high for 30 seconds. Add oil and swirl to coat skillet for 30 seconds longer. Add minced garlic, gingerroot, scallions, and salt. Stir-toss for 30 seconds.

3. Add tofu slices. Stir-toss for 2 minutes. Blend in seasoning and stir well. Cook for 30 seconds longer.

Transfer to serving platter. This dish goes well with rice or noodles, together with a salad or vegetable.

Yield: 4 servings

Seasoning

1 teaspoon cornstarch
½ teaspoon sugar
3 tablespoons cold water
2 tablespoons Worcestershire sauce
1 tablespoon soy sauce
1 tablespoon sesame seed oil

Ingredients

1 pound firm tofu, drained
3 tablespoons corn, vegetable, or safflower oil
1 teaspoon minced fresh garlic or (TS)
    2 large cloves garlic, finely minced
1 teaspoon grated fresh gingerroot (TS)
4 tablespoons diced fresh scallions (TS) or 2 scallions with green tops, diced
½ teaspoon salt

Equipment

measuring spoons
large spoon or spatula
cup or small bowl
10-inch skillet or 14-inch wok
Chinese cleaver or sharp knife
cutting board
grater
colander or strainer
tray for ingredients
serving platter

Tofu with Vegetables in Oyster Sauce

Seasoning

1 teaspoon sugar
1 teaspoon cornstarch
¼ teaspoon white pepper
¼ cup straw mushroom water
3 tablespoons oyster sauce
1 tablespoon sesame seed oil

Ingredients

½ can (16-ounces) straw
   mushrooms*
1 pound firm tofu, drained
3 tablespoons corn, vegetable, or
   safflower oil
½ cup sliced bamboo shoots
(TS) 4 tablespoons diced fresh scallions
   or 2 scallions with green tops,
   diced
1 teaspoon sesame seed oil

Equipment

measuring spoons and cups
large spoon or spatula
cup or small bowl
10-inch skillet or 14-inch wok
Chinese cleaver or sharp knife
cutting board
colander or strainer
tray for ingredients
serving platter

*For a fuller dish, use the entire 16-ounce can. Fresh or canned button mushrooms can be substituted, if preferred.

Unassuming but an unbelievably delicious dish that goes well with meat, poultry, or seafood. Oyster sauce blends well with tofu and adds a rich glaze to the dish.

Before you start

Drain straw mushrooms but save ¼ cup liquid to use in seasoning. Mix seasoning ingredients together in cup or small bowl.

1. Cut tofu into 1 x 1 x ⅛-inch slices. Drain in colander again to remove excess water. Set aside.

2. Heat skillet or wok on high for 30 seconds. Add oil and swirl to coat skillet for 30 seconds longer. Add bamboo shoots, straw mushrooms, and scallions. Stir-toss for 1 minute.

3. Add tofu slices and stir-toss for 2 minutes. Add seasoning ingredients, blend, and cook for 1 minute longer. Stir to blend well.

Remove to serving platter. Drizzle sesame oil on top of tofu and serve. This dish goes well with hot rice and another entree.

Yield: 4 servings

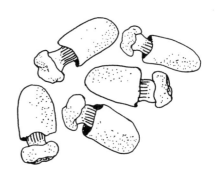

Ma Po Tofu

According to legend, this dish was invented by Chen Ma Po (Pock-marked Grandma Chen) in the city of Chengtu of Sichuan province. Ma Po owned a small eatery and was very fond of serving spicy dishes. Since then, this has become one of the more popular dishes in the highly spiced cuisine of Sichuan.

Before you start

Mix seasoning ingredients together in medium bowl.

1. Add ground pork to seasoning in bowl. Blend well and set aside.

2. Slice tofu into ½-inch cubes (p. 20). Drain in colander again to remove excess water. Set aside.

3. Heat skillet or wok on high for 30 seconds. Add oil and swirl to coat skillet for 30 seconds longer. Add Hunan chili paste and minced garlic. Stir-toss for 1 minute. Add pork mixture and stir-toss for 2 minutes longer.

4. Add sliced tofu and stir-toss for 2 minutes. Add diced scallions and mix well.

Serve over hot rice together with a salad or vegetable.

Note

For a milder taste, reduce the Hunan chili paste to 1 tablespoon. The amount of chili paste you use depends on how hot you like it: fiery hot (2 to 3 tablespoons), medium hot (1 to 1½ tablespoons), or mild (½ tablespoon). Different brands vary in intensity of hotness. Experiment for best results.

Yield: 4 servings

Seasoning

½ teaspoon cornstarch
¼ teaspoon sugar
¼ teaspoon black pepper
½ tablespoon soy sauce
½ teaspoon grated fresh
    gingerroot
½ tablespoon dry sherry, gin, or
    vodka, optional

Ingredients

¼ pound lean ground pork or
    ground beef
1 pound firm tofu, drained
3 tablespoons corn, vegetable, or
    safflower oil
1 to 1½ tablespoons Hunan or
    Chinese chili paste
1 teaspoon minced fresh garlic or (TS)
    2 large cloves garlic, finely minced
4 tablespoons fresh scallions or 2 (TS)
    scallions with green tops, diced

Equipment

measuring spoons
large spoon or spatula
medium bowl
10-inch skillet or 14-inch wok
Chinese cleaver or sharp knife or
    food processor
cutting board, grater
colander, serving platter
tray for ingredients

Just Spinach

—————◆—————

Dressing

½ teaspoon sugar

⅛ teaspoon salt

⅛ teaspoon black pepper

1 tablespoon sesame seed oil

½ tablespoon soy sauce

½ tablespoon white vinegar

(TS) ¼ teaspoon minced fresh garlic or 1 small clove garlic, finely minced

Ingredients

4 cups cold water

2 thin slices fresh gingerroot, each about the size of a 50-cent piece

1 pound fresh spinach

Equipment

measuring spoons and cups

wooden spoon

cup or small bowl

4-quart saucepot

Chinese cleaver or sharp knife

cutting board

colander or strainer

serving platter

Spinach with a new twist. It is as good as it is simple to make.

Before you start

Mix dressing in cup or small bowl.

1. Place 4 cups cold water in saucepot. Add gingerroot and bring to boil.

2. Wash and rinse spinach several times, taking care that all dirt has been rinsed off. Drain well.

3. Add spinach to boiling water and cook on high for no more than 30 seconds. Drain well. Discard gingerroot slices.

4. Transfer spinach to serving platter. Pour dressing over spinach and toss to coat thoroughly.

Serve hot or cold, together with a meat dish, accompanied by rice or noodles.

Note

The Chinese cooking term for this kind of parboiling is called "flying through water." No sooner is the vegetable dropped in boiling water than it is removed. The spinach is barely cooked, but the rawness is gone. The gingerroot also makes the spinach easier to digest. Do not use frozen spinach for this recipe because it does not have the same body and texture as fresh spinach.

Yield: 4 servings

The Chinese Cupboard

Chinese Gourmet Salad

Dragon and Phoenix in the Forest

Ants on the Hill

Floating Blossoms

Chinese Stir-Fry

Fish Steamed in Microwave

Litchis and Bubbles

Asparagus Salad

A special treat when asparagus are plentiful and in season. Gently parboiled or steamed, the asparagus are crisp and crunchy but not raw.

Before you start

Mix dressing ingredients in large bowl and set aside. Have boiling water ready.

1. Wash asparagus stalks and snap off tough ends. The stalks usually break at the woody part of the stem. Discard ends.

2. Slice stalks diagonally (p. 20) into 2-inch lengths. If you prefer the spears whole, do not cut.

3. Parboil asparagus in 2 quarts rapidly boiling water for 1 or 2 minutes or steam for 5 minutes in vegetable steamer.

4. Drain asparagus under cold running water to stop cooking process and help retain color.

5. Add asparagus to dressing in bowl. Toss to coat well.

   Serve immediately.

Note

Fresh asparagus is definitely better than frozen, for it is firm and crunchy. This salad can be made ahead of time and chilled in the refrigerator for several hours but do not add oyster sauce in dressing until serving time.

Yield: 4 servings

Dressing

$1/2$ teaspoon sugar
$1/4$ teaspoon white pepper
1 tablespoon soy sauce
1 tablespoon sesame seed oil
$1/2$ tablespoon oyster sauce

Ingredients

2 quarts boiling water
$1\frac{1}{2}$ pounds fresh asparagus or 2 packages (10-ounces each) frozen asparagus spears, well-thawed

Equipment

measuring spoons and cups
wooden spoon
large bowl
4-quart saucepot or vegetable steamer
Chinese cleaver or sharp knife
cutting board
colander or strainer
salad plates

Chinese Coleslaw

Dressing

2 teaspoons sugar
1 teaspoon Dijon mustard
¼ teaspoon salt
⅛ teaspoon black pepper
2 tablespoons wine vinegar
2 tablespoons soy sauce
1 tablespoon sesame seed oil
(TS) *1 teaspoon minced fresh garlic or 2 large cloves garlic, finely minced*

Ingredients

1 small head cabbage, about 1 pound
1 small carrot
(TS) *2 tablespoons diced fresh scallions or 1 scallion with green top, diced*

Equipment

measuring spoons
wooden spoon
chopsticks or fork
large bowl
Chinese cleaver or sharp knife
cutting board
grater or food processor with shredding blade
paring knife or peeler

A salad that doubles as a vegetable. It's very different from its Western cousin, but you'll like it even better. What's more, the flavor improves with age.

Before you start

Mix dressing ingredients together in large bowl until smooth.

1. Rinse cabbage. Cut in half, then into quarters. Cut and discard core. Cut each section in half, lengthwise. Shred cabbage on grater into very thin pieces. Or feed cabbage wedges one by one through food processor with shredder blade. Add cabbage to dressing ingredients in large bowl.

2. Pare carrot. Shred into thin pieces. Add carrot slivers to cabbage. Toss vegetables in bowl with dressing and mix well. Sprinkle diced scallions on top and mix gently. Chill well before serving.

Serve with an entree of your choice, together with rice or noodles.

Variation

You can make different variations by adding 4 to 6 ounces of thinly sliced meat from one of the following: Roast Pork (p. 24), No-work Chicken (p. 26), or Mandarin Roast Duck (p. 28). Top the salad with gravy from the meat. This salad can also be made ahead of time and refrigerated. Good for at least several days.

Yield: 4 to 6 servings

Zucchini, Carrot, and Agar-agar Salad

A salad out of the ordinary in its subtle combination of texture, color, and flavor. But it's good, it's different, and it's satisfying.

Before you start

Mix dressing ingredients together in large bowl until smooth.

1. Soak agar-agar strips in 2 cups of hot water in large bowl. Set aside.

2. Peel carrots and parboil in 2 cups boiling water. Cover and cook for 3 minutes. Drain and immediately refresh in cold water to stop cooking. Straight-slice into ⅛-inch rounds (p. 19). Set aside.

3. Wash zucchinis and cut diagonally into ¼-inch slices (p. 20). Stack slices and cut into julienne strips. Set aside.

4. Drain agar-agar strips. Add to dressing in bowl, together with carrots and zucchinis. Combine all ingredients and toss to blend well.

Serve with an entree of your choice, together with hot rice or noodles.

Note

Use only agar-agar strips, not agar-agar flakes or squares. Otherwise, you will not get the same results. Substitute seasonal vegetables of your choice for variety and color. Julienned ham, No-work Chicken (p. 26), or Mandarin Roast Duck (p. 28) can be added also. This salad can be made ahead of time and chilled for several hours before it is served.

Yield: 4 servings

Dressing

1 teaspoon sugar
⅛ teaspoon black pepper
2 tablespoons sesame seed oil
2 tablespoons wine vinegar
1 tablespoon soy sauce
1 tablespoon Worcestershire sauce

Ingredients

1 cup dried agar-agar strips, cut into 2-inch lengths
2 cups hot water
4 small carrots
2 cups boiling water
2 small zucchinis

Equipment

measuring spoons and cups
wooden spoon
2 large bowls
2-quart saucepot with lid
Chinese cleaver or sharp knife
cutting board
kitchen shears
paring knife or peeler
colander or strainer

Crunchy Noodle Salad

<hr>

Seasoning

½ teaspoon sugar
dash of black pepper
1 teaspoon sesame seed oil

Ingredients

1 package (5-ounces) cooked
    frozen salad baby shrimp
3 cups boiling water
4 small carrots
1 can (16-ounces) straw
    mushrooms
(TS) 3 cups fried cellophane
    noodles (p. 17)
1 cup Instant Sweet and Sour
    Sauce (p. 116), Instant Litchi
    Sauce (p. 116), or Tangy
    Pineapple Sauce (p. 117) as
    dressing*

Equipment

measuring spoons and cups
wooden spoon
cup or small bowl
medium bowl
2-quart saucepot with lid
Chinese cleaver or sharp knife
cutting board
colander or strainer
4 salad plates

*Your guests can have their pick if you
have all three sauces on hand. If not,
use your favorite American salad
dressing.*

An unusual salad—with a different combination of ingredients. Baby shrimp, carrots, straw mushrooms, and fried cellophane noodles come together to create a colorful, Chinese salad.

Before you start

Mix seasoning ingredients in cup or small bowl. Soak baby shrimp in 1 cup boiling water in medium bowl for 5 minutes.

1. Drain shrimp and add seasoning in bowl. Blend well and set aside.

2. Peel carrots and parboil in 2 cups boiling water. Cover and cook for 3 minutes. Drain and immediately refresh in cold water to stop cooking. Straight-slice into ⅛-inch rounds (p. 19). Set aside.

3. Drain straw mushrooms and divide into 4 portions. Set aside.

4. Line each of 4 salad plates with ¾ cup of deep-fried cellophane noodles. Top with carrot coins, then straw mushrooms. Place seasoned shrimp on top.

    Pass the dressing in a separate small bowl so that diners can add their own to the salad.

Note

Cellophane noodles, made from green mung beans, are very versatile. They can be served boiled or deep-fried. Deep-fried noodles can be stored in an air-tight container in a refrigerator for a week.

Yield: 4 servings

Chinese Gourmet Salad

Here's a salad bound to please. It's so good you can serve it as a main course at a luncheon. Beautiful to serve and definitely gourmet.

Before you start

Chill salad plates for 5 minutes.

1. Wash and rinse spinach several times to remove all dirt. Drain well and divide into 4 portions.

2. Line pre-chilled salad plates with spinach leaves. Top with fried cellophane noodles.

3. Divide straw mushrooms into 4 equal portions and spread one portion on top of noodles on each plate.

4. Cut eggs into quarters and place 4 pieces on top of each plate.

   Pass the dressing in a separate small bowl so that diners can add their own to the salad.

Variation

Diced cooked No-work Chicken (p. 26), or Mandarin Roast Duck (p. 28) can be added for a fuller dish.

Yield: 4 servings

Ingredients

1 pound leaf spinach
2 cups fried cellophane (TS)
  noodles (p. 17)
1 can (10-ounces) straw
  mushrooms
4 cooked Tea Eggs (p. 30), or 4 (S)
  hard-boiled eggs*
1 cup Instant Sweet and Sour
  Sauce (p. 116), Instant Litchi
  Sauce (p. 116), or Tangy
  Pineapple Sauce (p. 117)**

Equipment

measuring cups
wooden spoon
Chinese cleaver or sharp knife
cutting board
colander or strainer
4 salad plates

*Hard-boiled eggs may be substituted, but the salad will not be as tasty or gourmet.

**Your guests can have their pick if you have all three sauces on hand. If not, use your favorite American salad dressing.

Green Peppers

◆

Seasoning

1 tablespoon sugar
½ teaspoon black pepper
¼ cup soy sauce
¼ cup cold water
2 tablespoons dry sherry, gin, or
   vodka, optional

Ingredients

4 medium green peppers
3 tablespoons corn, vegetable, or
   safflower oil
(TS) 1 teaspoon minced fresh garlic or
   2 large cloves garlic, finely
   minced

Equipment

measuring spoons and cups
large spoon or spatula
cup or small bowl
10-inch skillet or 14-inch wok
   with lid
Chinese cleaver or sharp knife
cutting board
colander or strainer
serving platter or covered
   container

This dish is best enjoyed cold. Although it goes well as a vegetable served just after it has been cooked, it is also an attractive cold relish. The recipe was given to me by my maiden aunt who is now in her late 80s.

Before you start

Mix seasoning ingredients together in cup or small bowl and set aside.

1. Wash peppers and cut each in half, lengthwise. Scoop out seeds and cut off caps. Cut each half lengthwise into 4 segments. Rinse and drain well.

2. Heat skillet or wok on high for 30 seconds. Add oil and swirl to coat skillet for 30 seconds longer. Add garlic. Stir-toss for 30 seconds. Add pepper slices. Stir-toss for 1 minute, so that all segments are coated with oil. Add seasoning and bring to a boil.

3. Turn heat to medium low, cover, and cook for 4 minutes longer.

Transfer to serving platter. This dish goes well with a meat or poultry dish, together with hot rice.

Note

For a cold relish, spoon peppers and gravy into a covered container and refrigerate overnight. The flavor improves with aging. Green peppers can be enjoyed cold for up to a week when refrigerated.

Yield: 4 to 6 servings

Stir-fried Mushrooms and Bamboo Shoots

Mushroom and bamboo shoot lovers will appreciate this dish. Not too heavy but rich enough to satisfy.

1. Wash and quarter fresh mushrooms.

2. Heat skillet or wok on high for 30 seconds. Add oil and swirl to coat skillet for 30 seconds longer. Add garlic and salt. Stir-toss for 15 seconds.

3. Add fresh mushrooms, canned straw mushrooms, and bamboo shoots. Stir to coat evenly. Add sugar.

4. Continue cooking on high for 1 minute. Add water, cover, and steam on medium high for 2 minutes.

Transfer to serving platter. This dish goes well with Hong Kong Steak (p. 57) or Pepper Steak (p. 60) and hot rice.

Yield: 4 servings

Ingredients

½ pound fresh mushrooms
4 tablespoons corn, vegetable, or safflower oil
1 teaspoon minced fresh garlic or (TS) 2 large cloves garlic, finely minced
½ teaspoon salt
½ can (16-ounces) straw mushrooms
1 cup sliced bamboo shoots
½ teaspoon sugar
¼ cup water

Equipment

measuring spoons and cups
large spoon or spatula
10-inch skillet or 14-inch wok with lid
Chinese cleaver or sharp knife
cutting board
tray for ingredients
serving platter

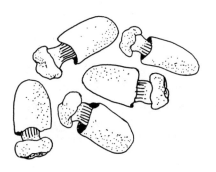

Stir-fried Green Beans, Sichuan Style

Seasoning

1 teaspoon cornstarch
½ teaspoon sugar
¼ teaspoon salt
¼ teaspoon black pepper
½ cup cold water
½ tablespoon soy sauce
½ teaspoon oyster sauce

Ingredients

1 pound fresh green beans, or 2
   packages (10-ounces each)
   frozen green beans, well-thawed
3 tablespoons corn, vegetable, or
   safflower oil
(TS) 1 teaspoon minced fresh garlic or
   2 large cloves garlic, minced
½ to 1 tablespoon Hunan chili
   paste or any brand of Chinese
   chili paste
2 tablespoons ground pork or
   ground beef

Equipment

measuring spoons and cups
large spoon or spatula
cup or small bowl
10-inch skillet or 14-inch wok
   with lid
Chinese cleaver or sharp knife
cutting board, kitchen shears
colander or strainer
tray for ingredients
serving platter

Stir-fried beans spiked with Hunan chili paste are a boon to spicy food fanciers. Try this dish when green beans are at their best and freshest.

Before you start

Mix seasoning ingredients in cup or small bowl.

1. Snip off top ends of green beans with kitchen shears, then cut in half. Wash and drain well. If using frozen beans, drain well and set aside.

2. Heat skillet or wok on high for 30 seconds. Add oil and swirl to coat skillet for 30 seconds longer. Add minced garlic, Hunan chili paste, and ground pork. Stir-toss for 30 seconds.

3. Add beans and stir-toss for 1 minute. Add seasoning. Turn heat to medium, cover, and steam for 4 to 5 minutes. If using frozen beans, reduce cooking time to half.

Spoon beans onto serving platter and serve, accompanied by a meat, poultry, or seafood dish together with hot rice or noodles.

Note

Omit the 2 tablespoons ground pork or ground beef if you prefer the dish meatless but follow the same cooking procedures. The amount of chili paste you use depends on how hot you like it: fiery hot (2 to 3 tablespoons), medium hot (1 to 1½ tablespoons), or mild (½ tablespoon). Different brands vary in intensity of hotness. Experiment for best results.

Yield: 4 to 6 servings

Peapods with Water Chestnuts and Straw Mushrooms

If you are fond of peapods, you'll love this dish. Accompanied by dainty straw mushrooms and crunchy water chestnuts, these peapods will delight the palate and please the eye.

Before you start

Mix seasoning ingredients in cup or small bowl.

1. With kitchen shears, snip off top end of fresh peapods. Wash and drain well. If using frozen peapods, thaw and drain well. Set aside.

2. Heat skillet or wok on high for 30 seconds. Add oil and swirl to coat skillet for 30 seconds longer. Add garlic. Stir-toss for 15 seconds.

3. Add peapods. Stir-toss for 1 minute. Add water chestnuts, straw mushrooms, and seasoning. Cover and cook for 1 minute.

   Transfer to serving platter. This dish goes well with a spicy entree and steamed rice.

Yield: 4 to 6 servings

Seasoning

½ teaspoon salt
½ teaspoon sugar
½ teaspoon cornstarch
⅛ teaspoon white pepper
¼ cup cold water

Ingredients

½ pound fresh edible peapods or 1 package (6-ounces) frozen peapods
3 tablespoons corn, vegetable, or safflower oil
½ teaspoon minced fresh garlic or (TS) 1 large clove garlic, finely minced
1 cup whole water chestnuts, drained
1 can (16-ounces) straw mushrooms, drained

Equipment

measuring spoons and cups
large spoon or spatula
cup or small bowl
10-inch skillet or 14-inch wok with lid
Chinese cleaver or sharp knife
cutting board
kitchen shears
colander or strainer
tray for ingredients
serving platter

Stir-fried Celery with Chinese Mushrooms

Seasoning

½ teaspoon sugar
¼ teaspoon salt
¼ teaspoon white pepper
½ cup mushroom water
1 teaspoon soy sauce
1 teaspoon sesame seed oil

Ingredients

(TS) 8 fresh shiitake mushrooms or 8
    small Chinese dried black
    mushrooms, presoaked (p. 16)
4 celery ribs
3 tablespoons corn, vegetable, or
    safflower oil

Equipment

measuring spoons and cups
large spoon or spatula
cup or small bowl
medium bowl
10-inch skillet or 14-inch wok
    with lid
Chinese cleaver or sharp knife
cutting board
tray for ingredients
serving platter

A contrast of texture and color. The sweet taste and velvety texture of black mushrooms blend well with crisp celery.

Before you start

Mix seasoning ingredients in cup or small bowl and set aside.

1. Wash fresh shiitake mushrooms. Cut off and discard stems. Cut caps into thin slices (p. 19). If using presoaked Chinese dried black mushrooms, squeeze dry. Cut off and discard stems. Cut caps into ¼-inch wide slices and set aside.

2. Wash celery and slice diagonally (p. 20) across celery ribs into ½-inch thick pieces. Set aside.

3. Heat skillet or wok on high for 30 seconds. Add oil and swirl to coat skillet for 30 seconds longer. Add mushrooms. Stir-toss for 1 minute. Add celery. Stir-toss for 1 minute.

4. Add seasoning and blend well. Cover and cook on medium heat for 4 minutes.

Spoon to serving platter and serve hot, together with a meat dish, accompanied by rice or noodles.

Variation

You can substitute ½ cup thin-sliced fresh mushrooms for either shiitake or Chinese dried black mushrooms.

Yield: 4 servings

Chinese Stir-fry

A marvelous combination of colors and a vegetarian's delight. If you are tired of the same old mixed vegetables, try this dish for taste and flavor.

Before you start

Mix seasoning ingredients in cup or small bowl.

1. Wash zucchini and yellow squash. Cut off both ends and discard. Cut diagonally into ¼-inch thick slices. Stack slices and cut into ¼-inch wide julienne strips (p. 20). Set aside on tray.

2. Cut off both ends of carrot and peel. Cut diagonally into ¼-inch slices. Stack slices and cut into ¼-inch wide julienne strips. Set aside on tray.

3. Heat skillet or wok on high for 30 seconds. Add oil and swirl to coat skillet for 30 seconds longer. Add garlic and carrots. Stir-toss for 1 minute.

4. Add seasoning to skillet and mix well. Cover and cook for 2 minutes. Add strips of zucchini and yellow squash to carrots. Stir-toss for 2 minutes.

   Spoon to serving platter and serve.

Yield: 4 servings

Seasoning

½ teaspoon salt
¼ teaspoon sugar
¼ teaspoon black pepper
½ cup cold water or freshly made (S)
    soup stock (p. 22–23)

Ingredients

1 medium zucchini
1 medium yellow squash
1 medium carrot
3 tablespoons corn, vegetable, or
    safflower oil
½ teaspoon minced fresh garlic or (TS)
    1 large clove garlic, finely
    minced

Equipment

measuring spoons and cups
large spoon or spatula
cup or small bowl
10-inch skillet or 14-inch wok
    with lid
Chinese cleaver or sharp knife
cutting board
paring knife or peeler
tray for ingredients
serving platter

Quick-cooked Rice

Ingredients
1 cup long grain white rice
1½ cups cold water

Equipment
measuring cups
1½-quart saucepot with lid
chopsticks or fork
serving bowl

To come up with a quick satisfying recipe for rice cooked the Chinese way was a challenge. The fiber of the rice kernel has to soften before it can be cooked. By soaking the rice in cold water for 8 hours or overnight, the kernels are soft enough to cook quickly.

1. Put rice in saucepot and rinse twice with cold water. Pour off excess water by cupping hand over rice grains.

2. Add cold water to rice in saucepot and let stand for 8 hours or overnight.

3. When you are ready to cook, bring rice to boil over high heat.

4. When water bubbles to top of saucepot in about 5 minutes, stir with chopsticks or fork to prevent sticking. Continue to cook on high until all the water is absorbed, in about 3 minutes.

5. Once crater holes appear on rice, and the water has evaporated, turn heat to simmer. Cover with a tight-fitting lid and steam for at least 7 minutes. Do not lift cover. Longer steaming time will yield fluffier rice.

6. After steaming is complete, uncover. Fluff rice with chopsticks or fork. Replace lid and let stand on stove until ready to serve.

Yield: 3½ cups

Fried Rice with Ham and Eggs

———— ◆ ————

All Chinese restaurants feature fried rice. Now you will find out how easy it is to cook for yourself.

Before you start

Separate kernels of cooked rice with your fingers and set aside.

1. Rinse peas and carrots under hot water for 1 minute. Drain well and set aside.

2. Heat skillet or wok on high for 30 seconds. Add 2 tablespoons oil and swirl to coat skillet for 1 minute longer. Add eggs and stir-fry until liquid is set but eggs are not dry or browned. Transfer cooked eggs to small bowl and break into small pieces with fork or chopsticks. Set aside.

3. Swirl remaining oil in hot skillet for 30 seconds. Add scallions, salt, and rice. Stir-toss for 1 minute. Turn heat to medium low and stir-toss for 2 minutes longer until all grains of rice are coated.

4. Add peas, carrots, and ham. Stir-toss for 2 to 3 minutes longer. Add eggs and mix well.

   Serve hot together with a soup, salad, or entree of your choice.

Note

Fried rice can be reheated in the oven at 250° for 15 minutes or in a microwave oven in a covered dish on high for 5 minutes.

Variation

Any cooked meat or poultry, finely diced, can be substituted for ham.

Yield: 4 to 6 servings

Ingredients

4 cups cooked long grain rice (S)
   (p. 32), cooked at least a day in
   advance
1 package (10-ounces) frozen peas
   and carrots, thawed
4 tablespoons corn, vegetable, or
   safflower oil, divided
2 eggs, well beaten and seasoned
   with dash of salt and white
   pepper
4 tablespoons diced fresh scallions (TS)
   or 2 scallions with green tops,
   diced
½ teaspoon salt
1 cup diced ham

Equipment

measuring spoons and cups
large spoon or spatula
2 small bowls
medium bowl
10-inch skillet or 14-inch wok
Chinese cleaver or sharp knife
cutting board
colander or strainer
tray for ingredients
chopsticks or fork

Vegetarian Fried Rice

Ingredients

(S) *4 cups cooked long grain rice
      (p. 32), cooked at least a day in
      advance*

  *1 package (10-ounces) frozen peas
      and carrots, well-thawed*

  *1 package (10-ounces) frozen
      whole kernel corn, well-thawed*

  *4 tablespoons corn, vegetable, or
      safflower oil, divided*

  *2 eggs, well beaten and seasoned
      with dash of salt and white
      pepper*

(TS) *4 tablespoons diced fresh scallions
      or 2 scallions with green tops,
      diced*

  ¼ teaspoon salt

  1 tablespoon soy sauce

  *1 can (4-ounces) button
      mushrooms or mushroom
      stems and pieces, drained*

Equipment

*measuring spoons and cups
large spoon or spatula
2 small bowls
medium bowl
10-inch skillet or 14-inch wok
Chinese cleaver or sharp knife
cutting board
large colander or strainer
tray for ingredients
chopsticks or fork*

Ever-popular fried rice with a twist—cooked with three kinds of vegetables. Truly a colorful and delicious meal-in-one.

Before you start

Separate kernels of cooked rice with your fingers and set aside.

1. Place frozen vegetables in large colander and rinse under hot water for 2 minutes. Drain well and set aside.

2. Heat skillet or wok on high for 30 seconds. Add 2 tablespoons oil and swirl to coat skillet for 1 minute longer. Add eggs and stir-fry until liquid is set, but eggs are not dry or browned. Transfer cooked eggs to small bowl and break into small pieces with chopsticks or fork. Set aside.

3. Swirl remaining oil in hot skillet for 30 seconds. Add scallions, salt, and rice. Stir-toss for 1 minute. Turn heat to medium low and stir-toss for 2 minutes longer until all grains of rice are coated with oil. Add soy sauce and blend well.

4. Add vegetables and mushrooms. Stir-toss for 3 minutes. Add eggs and mix well.

Serve hot with a soup, salad, or entree of your choice.

Note

Fried rice can be reheated in the oven at 250° for 15 minutes or in a microwave oven in a covered dish on high for 5 minutes.

Yield: 6 to 8 servings

Shrimp Fried Rice

No wonder Chinese fried rice is so popular! Especially Shrimp Fried Rice . . . which is so good and filling. Salt, instead of soy sauce, is used in this recipe.

Before you start

Mix seasoning ingredients together in small bowl. Soak shrimp in boiling water in medium bowl for 5 minutes. Drain. Separate kernels of cooked rice with your fingers. Rinse peas in hot water for 1 minute. Drain well.

1. Add seasoning ingredients to drained shrimp in medium bowl and mix together well. Set aside.

2. Heat skillet or wok on high for 30 seconds. Add 2 tablespoons oil and swirl to coat skillet for 1 minute longer. Add eggs and stir-toss until liquid is set, but eggs are not dry or browned. Transfer cooked eggs to small bowl and break into small pieces with chopsticks or fork. Set aside.

3. Swirl 2 tablespoons oil in hot skillet for 30 seconds. Add scallions, salt, and rice. Stir-toss for 1 minute. Turn heat to medium low and stir-toss for 2 minutes longer until all grains of rice are coated.

4. Add peas and stir-toss for 2 minutes longer. Add eggs and shrimp. Mix well.

Serve hot together with a soup, salad, or entree of your choice.

Note

Fried rice can be reheated in the oven at 250° for 15 minutes or in a microwave oven in a covered dish on high for 5 minutes.

Yield: 4 to 6 servings

Seasoning

¼ teaspoon white pepper
¼ teaspoon sugar
¼ teaspoon salt
1 teaspoon sesame seed oil

Ingredients

1 package (5-ounces) frozen
    cooked baby shrimp
2 cups boiling water
4 cups cooked long grain rice (S)
    (p. 32), cooked at least a day in
    advance
1 package (10-ounces) frozen
    green peas, thawed
4 tablespoons corn, vegetable, or
    safflower oil, divided
2 eggs, well beaten, and seasoned
    with dash of salt and white
    pepper
4 tablespoons fresh scallions or 2 (TS)
    scallions with green tops, diced
½ teaspoon salt

Equipment

measuring spoons and cups
large spoon or spatula
2 small bowls
2 medium bowls
10-inch skillet or 14-inch wok
Chinese cleaver or sharp knife
cutting board
colander or strainer
tray for ingredients
chopsticks or fork

Roast Pork Fried Rice

Ingredients

4 cups cooked long grain rice
  (p. 32), cooked at least a day
  in advance

1 package (10-ounces) frozen
  peas, thawed

(S) 1 strip roast pork (p. 20), about
  ¼ pound

4 tablespoons corn, vegetable, or
  safflower oil, divided

2 eggs, well beaten and seasoned
  with dash of salt and white
  pepper

(TS) 4 tablespoons diced fresh scallions
  or 2 scallions with green tops,
  diced

½ teaspoon salt

(S) ¼ cup roast pork gravy (p. 25)

Equipment

measuring spoons and cups
large spoon or spatula
2 small bowls
medium bowl
10-inch skillet or 14-inch wok
Chinese cleaver or sharp knife
cutting board
colander or strainer
tray for ingredients
chopsticks or fork

Another variation on the popular fried rice, using roast pork.

Before you start

Separate kernels of cooked rice with your fingers and set aside. Rinse peas in hot water for 1 minute. Drain well.

1. Cut roast pork diagonally into ¼-inch wide slices (p. 20). Stack slices and cut into ¼-inch wide wide strips, then into pea-size pieces. Set aside.

2. Heat skillet or wok on high for 30 seconds. Add 2 tablespoons oil and swirl to coat skillet for 1 minute longer. Add eggs and stir-toss until liquid is set, but eggs are not dry or browned. Transfer cooked eggs to small bowl and break into small pieces with chopsticks or fork. Set aside.

3. Swirl 2 tablespoons oil in hot skillet for 30 seconds. Add scallions, salt, and rice. Stir-toss for 1 minute. Turn heat to medium and stir-toss for 1 minute longer until all grains of rice are coated with oil.

4. Add peas, roast pork, and roast pork gravy. Stir-toss for 2 minutes longer. Add eggs. Mix well.

Serve hot together with a soup, salad, or entree of your choice.

Note

Fried rice can be reheated in the oven at 250° for 15 minutes or in a microwave oven in a covered dish on high for 5 minutes.

Yield: 4 to 6 servings

Chinese Vegetable Rice

A simple combination of tastes. Stir-fried vegetables mixed with white rice. Different—but a winner every time!

Before you start

Separate kernels of cooked rice with your fingers and set aside. Mix seasoning ingredients in small cup or bowl.

1. Wash Napa cabbage and cut crosswise into ½-inch wide strips. Peel onion, cut off both ends, and thin-slice (p. 19). Wash mushrooms and thin-slice. Place vegetables in separate piles on tray. If using frozen spinach, drain well.

2. Heat skillet or wok on high for 30 seconds. Add oil and swirl to coat skillet for 30 seconds longer. Add garlic. Stir-toss for 15 seconds. Add onion: Stir-toss for 1 minute. Add mushrooms and stir-toss for 1 minute longer. Add Napa cabbage. Stir-toss for 1 minute. Add seasoning and blend well. Cover and cook on medium heat for 4 minutes longer.

Add cooked rice and blend well for 1 minute.

   Serve hot, together with a meat, seafood, or tofu dish of your choice.

Variation

If you have time and prefer to use freshly cooked rice, prepare rice according to directions on p. 32. While rice is steaming in covered pot, follow steps 1 to 3 above. Fresh or frozen chopped chard or collard greens can be substituted for the Napa cabbage, if preferred.

Yield: 4 to 6 servings.

Seasoning

½ teaspoon salt
½ teaspoon sugar
¼ teaspoon black pepper
2 teaspoons cold water

Ingredients

4 cups cooked long grain rice (S)
   (p. 32), cooked at least a day in
   advance
½ pound Napa cabbage, or 1
   package (10-ounces) chopped
   frozen spinach, well-thawed
1 large onion
6 medium fresh mushrooms
3 tablespoons corn, vegetable, or
   safflower oil
½ teaspoon minced fresh garlic or (TS)
   1 large clove garlic, finely
   minced

Equipment

measuring spoons and cups
large spoon or spatula
small cup or bowl
10-inch skillet or 14-inch wok
   with lid
Chinese cleaver or sharp knife
cutting board
tray for ingredients

Cold-tossed Noodles with Bean Sprouts

<hr>

Seasoning

1 tablespoon soy sauce

1 tablespoon sesame seed oil

1 tablespoon Hunan chili paste, or any brand of Chinese chili paste, optional*

1 teaspoon wine vinegar

(TS) *4 tablespoons diced fresh scallions or 2 scallions with green tops, diced*

(TS) *1 teaspoon minced fresh garlic or 2 large cloves garlic, finely minced*

Marinade

1 tablespoon sesame seed oil

½ teaspoon sugar

½ teaspoon salt

¼ teaspoon white pepper

Ingredients

large kettle boiling water

½ pound very thin noodles, fresh or dried

½ pound fresh bean sprouts, or 1 can (14-ounces) bean sprouts

A noodle dish that is made-to-order for lunch, brunch, or midnight snack, served hot or cold. It's a wonderful complement to a meat, chicken, or vegetable dish.

Before you start

Mix seasoning ingredients together in large bowl. Mix marinade ingredients together in medium bowl.

1. Cook noodles according to package directions until just tender (*al dente*). Rinse in cold water and drain well. Add noodles to seasoning in bowl and toss to coat well. Set aside.

2. While noodles are cooking, add 3 cups boiling water to 2-quart saucepot. Add bean sprouts and parboil for no more than 15 seconds. Drain under cold water. Add bean sprouts to marinade ingredients in bowl and toss to coat well. For canned bean sprouts, drain well, then add to marinade in bowl. Toss to coat well.

3. Add marinated bean sprouts to seasoned noodles. Mix together well.

   Spoon to serving platter.

Variation

The noodles may also be served plain without bean sprouts or substitute 1 to 2 tablespoons oyster sauce for the Hunan chili paste. Another variation is to substitute a raw cucumber, sliced into thin slivers, for the bean sprouts. Top it with sliced No-work Chicken (p. 26), Mandarin Roast Duck (p. 28) or Roast Pork (p. 24).

Yield: 4 to 6 servings

Equipment

measuring spoons and cups
large spoon
large bowl
medium bowl
4-quart saucepot with lid
2-quart saucepot with lid
Chinese cleaver or sharp knife
cutting board
2 colanders or strainers
tray for ingredients
serving platter

*The amount of chili paste you use depends on how hot you like it: fiery hot (2 to 3 tablespoons), medium hot (1 to 1½ tablespoons), or mild (½ tablespoon). Different brands vary in intensity of hotness. Experiment for best results.

Noodles in Soup

Ingredients

½ pound very thin noodles, fresh or dried

2 cups fresh spinach or 1 package (10-ounces) frozen leaf spinach

(S) *4 cups chicken soup stock, freshly made (p. 22), or 4 cups canned chicken broth**

2 quarts cold water

½ pound cooked ham, thinly sliced into strips

salt and pepper to taste

Equipment

measuring cups
large spoon
2 medium bowls
4-quart saucepot with lid
Chinese cleaver or sharp knife
cutting board
colander or strainer
chopsticks or fork
ladle
4 large soup bowls

*For a vegetarian dish, use vegetarian soup stock (p. 23).

A one-dish meal, as warm and satisfying as mother's chicken soup. Ideal for lunch or a late night snack, especially during the cold winter months.

Before you start

Cook noodles in 2 qts. cold water according to package directions until just tender. Drain and rinse under cold running water. Set aside.

1. Wash and rinse spinach several times, taking care that all dirt has been rinsed off. Drain well. If using frozen leaf spinach, just make sure it is well-thawed. Set aside.

2. Add soup stock to saucepot and bring to boil. Add spinach and cook for 3 minutes.

3. Add noodles. Reduce heat to low and simmer, covered, for 3 minutes.

4. Spoon noodles with spinach and broth into individual soup bowls. Garnish with sliced ham on top of noodles.

Serve immediately. Diners add their own salt and pepper to taste.

Variation

Sliced lettuce, Napa cabbage, or bok choy can be substituted for spinach. No-work Chicken (p. 26), Mandarin Roast Duck (p. 28), or Roast Pork (p. 24) can be used for garnish instead of ham.

Yield: 4 to 6 servings

Litchis and Bubbles

A simple elegant dessert, perfect with any meal. Serve it in your favorite stemware to your favorite VIPs.

Before you start

1. Wash and hull strawberries. Do not slice. Add sugar to strawberries and toss gently. Divide into 4 portions and set aside.

2. Divide litchis into 4 portions. Set aside.

3. Fill each glass with 1 portion each of strawberries and litchis. Alternate the fruits so that the red and white contrast with each other.

4. Fill with champagne or 7-Up. Garnish each glass with a sprig of mint.

Serve while the drink fizzes.

Yield: 4 servings

Ingredients

1 pint fresh strawberries
2 teaspoons sugar, optional
1 can (20-ounces) litchis, drained
1 bottle chilled champagne or 1
    quart chilled regular or diet
    7-Up
4 sprigs of fresh mint

Equipment

measuring spoons
small knife
cutting board
colander or strainer
tray for ingredients
4 champagne glasses or goblets

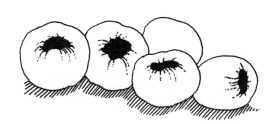

Chinese Fruit Melange

◆

Ingredients

1 can (20-ounces) litchis with
   juice
1 can (16-ounces) mandarin
   oranges with juice
1 pint fresh strawberries
fresh mint leaves for garnish

Equipment

large spoon
large bowl
small knife
cutting board
dessert bowls

A simple but perfectly light dessert. Luscious litchis, once favored by the beautiful Yang Kwei-Fei, favorite concubine of Emperor Tang, are combined with mandarin oranges and sweet strawberries—a perfect ending to a delicious meal.

Before you start

Chill cans of fruit in refrigerator several hours or overnight.

1. Wash, hull, and slice strawberries.

2. Just before serving, pour canned fruits with juice into large bowl. Add sliced strawberries. Mix fruits together.

Spoon fruit mixture with juices into dessert bowls, garnish with mint leaves, and serve.

Note

Combining ingredients just before serving preserves the integrity of each fruit. If preferred, fresh melon balls of any kind may be added or substituted successfully.

Yield: 4 to 6 servings

Litchi Ambrosia

This exotic drink will delight your guests. You won't believe how refreshing this is until you try it. A genuine Chinese-American creation which combines Chinese litchis with an American soft drink.

Before you start

Chill metal bowl in freezer for 3 minutes.

1. Place litchis and juice, ice cream, eggs, 7-Up, and almond extract in blender. Mix ingredients on low for 4 minutes.

2. Pour whipping cream into chilled metal bowl. Beat in mixer on high for 1 to 2 minutes until the cream is whipped into soft peaks.

3. Add whipped cream to contents in blender and blend on high for 2 minutes.

   Serve immediately in tall glasses.

Note

If made ahead of time for company, the drink is still delicious, but the zip that comes with freshly whipped shakes is missing.

Yield: 4 to 6 servings

Ingredients

1 can (20-ounces) litchis with
   juice
1 cup vanilla ice cream
2 eggs at room temperature
1 cup regular or diet 7-Up
1 tablespoon almond extract
¼ pint fresh whipping cream

Equipment

measuring spoons and cups
small metal bowl
electric mixer or egg beater
electric blender
tall glasses

Almond Fruit Float

———— ◆ ————

Ingredients

1½ cups cold milk
3 packages (¼-ounce each)
   unflavored gelatin
6 tablespoons sugar
1 tablespoon almond extract
1½ cups boiling water
1 can (20-ounces) litchis with
   juice, chilled
1 can (10-ounces) mandarin
   oranges with juice, chilled
6 to 8 red maraschino cherries for
   color

Equipment

measuring spoons and cups
large spoon
large bowl
electric blender
knife
9-inch square plastic container
   with lid
dessert bowls

A dessert the Chinese hold dear . . . and small wonder! It is light and refreshing with the addition of fresh fruit. It couldn't be better.

1. Add milk, gelatin, sugar, and almond extract in blender. Blend on high for 1 minute. Pour into plastic container.

2. Add boiling water to gelatin mixture. Mix well.

3. Cover, and refrigerate for about 4 hours or overnight, until mixture is firmly set.

4. Cut gelatin into diamond shapes by slicing diagonally in both directions. Spoon into dessert bowls.

5. Combine fruits in large bowl with juice. Spoon over gelatin diamonds.

   Serve.

Note

This dessert may be made ahead of time and refrigerated for several days. Fresh fruits in season (pineapple, berries, melons) as well as other canned fruits may be substituted.

Yield: 6 to 8 servings

Coconut Delight

———— ◆ ————

Light and exotic for summer or anytime. Agar-agar strips are used as the gelatin base. Once jelled, it will not dissolve, even at room temperature.

1. Place agar-agar strips in saucepot and add cold water. Bring mixture to a boil over high heat, about 7 minutes. Turn heat to medium and continue to cook until agar-agar strips are completely dissolved, about 8 minutes. Stir mixture several times to make sure that agar-agar does not stick to bottom of pot. Add sugar to mixture and blend well.

2. While agar-agar is cooking, pour evaporated milk and coconut cream into blender. Blend on high for about 1 minute. Pour mixture into plastic container.

3. Add agar-agar mixture to container and mix well.

4. Refrigerate until firm, about 2½ hours.

5. Cut Coconut Delight into large diamonds or squares and top with strawberry slices.

Alternate method of serving

Pour mixture into stemmed dessert dishes. Refrigerate until firm. Served in individual dishes, this dessert takes less time to chill. Top with sliced strawberries.

Note

It is important to use agar-agar strips, not agar-agar flakes or squares.

Yield: 10 to 12 servings

Ingredients

1½ cups (½-ounce) dried agar-agar strips, cut into 1-inch lengths

5 cups (2½ pints) cold water

4 tablespoons sugar

1 can (13-ounces) evaporated milk

1 can (15-ounces) coconut cream

1 cup sliced fresh strawberries or any fresh fruit in season

Equipment

measuring spoons and cups

large spoon

4-quart saucepot

electric blender

9-inch square plastic container with lid or 10 to 12 stemmed dessert dishes

rubber spatula

kitchen shears

doilies, if served in stemmed dishes

Hot Fruit Compote with Tofu

◆

Ingredients

8 ounces firm tofu, well drained
1 medium firm apple, preferably
    Granny Smith
1 tablespoon unsalted butter
½ teaspoon grated orange peel
(TS) ½ teaspoon grated gingerroot
1 cup sliced fresh strawberries,
    washed and hulled
1 tablespoon honey*
4 to 6 whole strawberries for
    garnish

Equipment

measuring spoons and cups
large spoon or spatula
10-inch skillet or 14-inch wok
    with lid
Chinese cleaver or sharp knife
cutting board
grater
colander or strainer
4 dessert dishes

*Add more honey if you prefer a
sweeter taste.

A dessert combining tofu with apple and strawberries, especially appealing to tofu aficionados.

1. Cut drained tofu into ½ x 1 x ½-inch thick cubes. Set aside.

2. Wash apple but do not peel. Quarter apple and cut off core. Cut each quarter into two slices lengthwise. Cut each slice into 4 cubed pieces. Set aside.

3. Heat skillet or wok on high for 30 seconds. Add butter and melt. Swirl melted butter to coat bottom of skillet evenly. Turn heat to medium.

4. Add tofu cubes and stir-toss for 1 to 2 minutes over medium heat.

5. Add cubed apple, grated orange peel, and grated gingerroot. Stir-toss for 30 seconds to blend well. Cover skillet, turn heat to low, and simmer tofu-apple mixture on low heat for 2 minutes.

6. Remove skillet from heat. Add sliced strawberries. Drizzle honey over tofu-fruit mixture in skillet. Stir gently to blend honey into mixture.

7. Spoon into individual dessert dishes. Garnish with a whole strawberry.

Variation

Substitute one firm, ripe, unpeeled pear for apple.

Yield: 4 servings

Strawberry and Tofu Pudding

A good way to enjoy summer fruits is to make fruit pudding. Here is a colorful dessert that is as flavorful as it is satisfying. Fresh strawberries are combined with tofu, a low-calorie, nutritious substitute for heavy cream or half-and-half cream.

Before you start

Chill metal bowl in freezer for 5 minutes.

1. Hull, wash, and drain strawberries. Halve or quarter larger ones. Reserve a few whole strawberries with stems for garnishing if you do not have mint sprigs.

2. Place strawberries, lemon juice, tofu, and sugar in food processor or blender. Puree on high until smooth, about 1 minute. Transfer puree to large bowl and set aside. You should have about 3 cups of strawberry-tofu mixture.

3. Add egg whites and cream of tartar to metal bowl. Beat on high until egg whites are stiff but not dry, about 2 minutes.

4. Fold egg whites into strawberry-tofu mixture. Spoon mixture into individual dessert or parfait glasses.

5. Chill in refrigerator for several hours or overnight.

Serve with a mint sprig or whole strawberry in each glass.

Note

Any fruit in season, such as blueberries or raspberries, can be substituted for the strawberries.

Yield: 4 to 6 servings

Ingredients

1 pint fresh ripe strawberries
juice of ½ lemon
½ pound soft tofu, well drained
½ cup sugar
2 egg whites at room temperature
½ teaspoon cream of tartar
4 to 6 fresh mint sprigs or stemmed whole strawberries for garnish

Equipment

measuring spoons and cups
large spoon
small metal bowl
large bowl
food processor or blender
electric mixer
small knife
rubber scraper
colander or strainer
dessert or parfait glasses

Instant Sweet and Sour Sauce

————————◆————————

Ingredients

¼ cup apricot preserves
¼ cup orange marmalade
¼ cup white vinegar
2 tablespoons ketchup
⅛ teaspoon salt
dash of white pepper

Equipment

measuring spoons and cups
blender
rubber spatula
covered jar or small bowl

Combine ingredients in blender and fine-chop for about 1 minute.

Yield: 1 cup

Instant Litchi Sauce

————————◆————————

Ingredients

½ (20-ounces) can litchis, drained
6 maraschino cherries
2 tablespoons white vinegar
2 teaspoons sugar

Equipment

measuring spoons
blender
rubber spatula
covered jar or small bowl

Combine ingredients in blender and fine-chop for about 1 minute.

Yield: 1 cup

Tangy Pineapple Sauce

Mix ingredients together in skillet and cook on medium heat. Stir constantly to prevent scorching. In about 3 minutes, mixture will thicken and come to a boil. Spoon into bowl or gravy boat. Leftover sauce can be stored in refrigerator in a covered jar or plastic container and reused.

Yield: 3 cups

Ingredients

*1 can (10-ounces) crushed
   pineapple with juice*
⅓ cup cider vinegar
½ cup white sugar
1 can (6-ounces) tomato paste
1 tablespoon cornstarch
½ cup water
1 small onion, finely minced

Equipment

measuring spoons and cups
large spoon or spatula
10-inch skillet or 14-inch wok
medium bowl or gravy boat

◈ *Tea* ◈

Tea is China's national drink and is served all the time—morning, noon, or night. It is also served before and after meals but seldom during meals (except in restaurants), as soup takes the place of tea. It is taken plain and undiluted, without sugar, lemon, milk, or cream.

The three main categories of tea are *green tea* (unfermented), *black or red tea* (fermented), and *oolong tea* (semi-fermented).

Green tea produces a light golden brew, with whole leaves that retain their natural green color. The taste is delicate. It is usually a higher grade tea and comes two ways, scented with dried blossoms or unscented. Black or red tea produces a full-bodied brew and since the tea is an inferior grade, the leaves are usually broken. Oolong tea, which produces an amber brew, is a cross between the black and green teas.

Selecting a tea depends on your preferences. I recommend trying all three kinds to decide which you like best. Lung Jin (Dragon Well) from Hangzhou is world-renowned green tea and Jasmine is also famous. Keemun is a good grade of red tea. Litchi and Kwan Yin teas are fragrant and popular, while Po Lei (Pu Erh), a soothing blend that aids in digestion, is one of my favorites.

To make a good pot of tea:
1. Use a porcelain or earthenware teapot, not metal.
2. Fill a clean kettle with fresh clean water.
3. When the water comes to a rolling boil, turn heat down.
4. Rinse out the teapot with hot water from kettle.
5. Measure about 1 teaspoon dried leaves (or 1 teabag) per cup. Place in warmed teapot. Add boiling water. Cover and let stand. Infusion starts when the leaves open.
6. Allow tea to steep for 3 to 5 minutes, then serve.
   A second or third infusion is equally delicious.
   Tea should be served with family and friends for complete enjoyment. To the Chinese, the essence of a blessed life is good friends, cups of good tea, and lively conversation.

◈ *Wines and Chinese Food* ◈

D. T. LONGONE

Wine is a classic Chinese beverage, used both in cooking and to accompany the meal. Traditional Chinese wines are made from grains, particularly rice, and are often flavored with herb or fruits. Generally they are served hot.

In the United States, Chinese wines are not widely available. More important, they are likely to be less appealing to Westerners accustomed only to grape wines. You might substitute a medium-dry sherry served warm in small cups, to be sipped throughout the meal. For spicier dishes, a medium-dry (not sweet) oloroso sherry provides an appropriate pungency. An interesting variation is to serve both sherries in the order given, with the oloroso for the main dish.

Matching American and European table wines with the range of dishes offered in this book presents a challenge. The usual guidelines —white wine with fish, fowl, and lighter dishes, red wine with meat —are less useful with Chinese dishes. A given course, fish, fowl, or meat, may range in character from the delicate to the pungent to the spicy hot. Let the details of sauce and spicing determine the most compatible wine. Although tea or beer may be more conventionally acceptable, a well-chosen wine can bring out hidden flavors and nuances. The selection and use of wine offers an additional culinary variation to the adventuresome cook.

Most vegetable, seafood, and poultry dishes are complemented by a fresh, dry, white wine. Try Chenin Blanc, Chardonnay, or Reisling and, from France, a Macon or Graves. These wines are also suitable with pork as are the slightly sweet Rhine and Moselle wines of the spätlese type from Germany.

Roast Duck is splendid with a fruity, red wine such as a light Zinfandel or, from France, a young Côtes du Rhone or Beaujolais.

Beef and spicy main dishes in general require a full-bodied red wine. A good choice is a California Cabernet. Perhaps still better would be a French bottle, either Bordeaux, Burgundy, or a better Beaujolais, such as one from Morgan or Moulin-à-Vent.

The guidelines above should serve only as a starting point for you.

3

HOW TO PLAN
A CHINESE MEAL

Planning a good Chinese meal is a skill that you can easily learn. A Chinese meal is based on principles of balance, the balance of flavors and textures, of *fan* and *ts'ai.*

Fan is the starch conponent. Literally it means "cooked rice," but it can also be steamed bread made from wheat, millet, or corn flour, pancakes, noodles, or wontons. *Ts'ai* is the word for vegetables. Whether the vegetables are cooked separately or cooked with meat together in one dish, or whether there are several entrees of meat, seafood, or poultry, all fall into the *ts'ai* category.

A Chinese meal is a communal meal of several dishes shared by everyone. It is not customary in China to cook the same dish and serve it on separate plates to each diner, nor is it common practice to cook a specific dish for each person. However, because there are so many ingredients and sauces, cutting and cooking methods, it is easy for a cook to serve a variety of dishes at a meal.

The following is a simple key to a successful planning of a Chinese meal. The result will be a well-balanced meal.

- Cook dishes according to the number of people in the party; usually one dish per person.
- Select a dish from each of the following categories: meat or poultry, seafood, eggs or tofu, and vegetables.
- Select a variety of cooking methods.
- Select according to the sauces and spices used.

4

SUGGESTED MENUS

The following menus can serve 4 or 6, depending on the appetite of your family and friends. Each portion of meat, poultry, and seafood is small, usually no more than 4 ounces.

Chinese-American Sandwiches

Chinese Meat Patties in hamburger buns, p. 52

Roast Pork (thinly sliced) with gravy in pita bread, p. 24

Light Lunches

Chinese Gourmet Salad, p. 91
Strawberry and Tofu Pudding, p. 115

Tomato and Egg Soup, p. 48
Shrimp Fried Rice, p. 103

Soup and Salad

Hot and Sour Soup, p. 51
Lettuce Rolls, p. 44

Floating Blossoms, p. 49
Crunchy Noodle Salad, p. 90

Vegetarian Lunches

Tofu with Spinach Soup, p. 47
Cold-tossed Noodles with Bean Sprouts, p. 106

Zucchini, Carrot, and Agar-agar Salad, p. 89
Chinese Vegetable Rice, p. 105

Winter Cocktail Party

Shrimp Chips, p. 34
Golden Wontons, p. 38
Shrimp Toast, p. 36
Beef on a Stick, p. 35

Summer Cocktail Party

Shrimp Chips, p. 34
Sesame Pork Balls, p. 37
Lettuce Rolls, p. 44

Dinner for Spring

Beef on a Stick, p. 35
Tofu with Spinach Soup, p. 47
Stir-fried Sichuan Shrimp, p. 79
Asparagus Salad, p. 87
Steamed Rice, p. 32
Chinese Fruit Melange, p. 110

Dinner for Summer

Cucumber Soup, p. 46
Pepper Steak, p. 60
Tofu with Three Spices, p. 83
Chinese Stir-fry, p. 99
Steamed Rice, p. 32
Coconut Delight, p. 113

Dinner for Fall

Tomato and Egg Soup, p. 48
Roast Pork with Tofu, p. 64
Shrimp in the Shell with Spicy Sauce, p. 78
Crunchy Broccoli, p. 94
Steamed Rice, p. 32
Almond Cookies, p. 33

Dinner for Winter

Baroque Pearls, p. 61
Hot and Sour Soup, p. 51
Turkey with Zucchini, p. 67
Pickled Spicy Cabbage, p. 31
Steamed Rice, p. 32
Almond Fruit Float, p. 112

Candlelight Dinner for VIPs

Floating Blossoms, p. 49
Mandarin Roast Duck, p. 28
Shrimp Steamed in the Shell, p. 73
Peapods with Water Chestnuts and Straw
  Mushrooms, p. 97
Steamed Rice, p. 32
Litchis and Bubbles, p. 107

Dinner for Sichuan Aficionados

Hot and Sour Soup, p. 51
Spicy Chicken with Cashews, p. 70
Stir-fried Sichuan Shrimp, p. 79
Stir-fried Green Beans, Sichuan Style, p. 96
Steamed Rice, p. 32
Litchi Ambrosia, p. 111

Vegetarian Dinner #1

Cucumber Soup (made with vegetable soup
  stock), p. 46
Tofu with Three Spices, p. 47
Bean Sprout Pancakes, p. 82
Vegetarian Fried Rice, p. 102
Almond Fruit Float, p. 112

Vegetarian Dinner #2

Tomato and Egg Soup (made with vegetable
  soup stock), p. 48
Egg Pouch, p. 81
Stir-fried Green Beans, Sichuan Style, p. 96
Steamed Rice, p. 32
Litchis and Bubbles, p. 107

STORES FOR CHINESE INGREDIENTS IN NORTH AMERICA

Most of the 12 Chinese ingredients are available from your local supermarkets or specialty stores. If not, check the yellow pages in your area for a Chinese or oriental food supply market. Otherwise, call or write to the store closest to your area, and order the needed items. Stores marked with an asterisk (*) will handle mail orders, either COD or with a prepaid check.

California

*Main On Food Corporation
6625 E. Washington Blvd.,
Los Angeles, CA 90040 (213-727-7100)

*Williams-Sonoma
576 Sutter Street
San Francisco, CA 94102 (415-982-6589)

*Wing Sing Chong Co., Inc.
685 7th Street
San Francisco, CA 94103 (415-982-4171)

Colorado

*Pacific Mercantile Company
1925 Lawrence Street
Denver, CO 80202 (303-295-0293)

Washington D.C.

*Gourmet
538 23rd St., at Virginia Ave., N.W.
Washington, D.C. 20037 (202-887-8240)

*Oriental Market
891-F Rockville Pike
Rockville, MD 20852 (301-340-8018)

Florida

Num Fong Produce and Oriental Food Supplies
355 N. E. 72 Terrace
Miami, FL 33138 (305-759-1398)

Georgia

*Chan and Chan Market
3275 Chamblee Dunwoody Road
Atlanta, GA 30341 (404-458-6838)

Michigan

*Asia Trading Company
734 S. Washington Avenue
Royal Oak, MI 48067 (313-543-9000)

Minnesota

*Kwong Tung Foods, Inc.
1840 E. 38th Street
Minneapolis, MN 55407 (612-722-9501)

Missouri

*Asian Food Products
3604–6 S. Grand Blvd.,
St. Louis, MO 63118 (314-935-4100)

New York

Kam Kuo Food, Inc.
7 Mott Street
New York, NY 10013 (212-349-3097)

Texas

Diho Supermarket
9280 Bellaire Blvd.,
Houston, TX 77036 (713-988-1881)

Terrace Oriental Market
400 N. Greenville Avenue
Richardson, TX 75081 (214-681-9313)

Washington

*Asian Connection
409 Maynard Ave. S., Suite 108
Seattle, WA 98104 (206-587-6010)

Canada

*Leong Jung Company
999 Clark Street
Montreal, Quebec
Canada H2Z 1K1 (514-861-9747)

Tai Ping Mart
484 Dundas Street W.
Toronto, Ontario
Canada M5T 1G9 (416-977-2462)

*Tech Shun Trading Co. Ltd.
138 E. Pender Street
Vancouver, British Columbia
Canada V6A 1T6 (604-684-5522)

◇ *Mail-order Form for Chinese Ingredients* ◇

Agar-agar strips 大膠菜

Cellophane noodles (bean thread or transparent noodles) 粉絲

Chinese dried black mushrooms 冬菇

Crunchy mushrooms (won yee or cloud ears) 雲耳

Five-spice powder 五香粉

Hoisin sauce 海鮮醬

Hunan chili paste 湖南辣椒醬

Litchis, canned 荔枝

Oyster sauce 蠔油

Sesame seed oil 蘇油

Shrimp chips 蝦片

Straw mushrooms, canned 草菇

INDEX

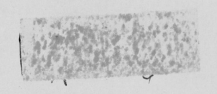